Everyday
Grilling

Everyday Grilling
© 2006 by Oxmoor House, Inc.
Book Division of Southern Progress Corporation
P.O. Box 2262, Birmingham, Alabama 35201-2262

For more information about *Southern Living* AT HOME®,
please write to:
Consultant Support
P.O. Box 830951
Birmingham, Alabama 35283-8309

ISBN: 0-8487-3129-8
Printed in the United States of America
First Printing 2006
Parts of this publication were previously published
as *Weber Grilling with Family & Friends*

Southern Living **At HOME**®

SENIOR VICE PRESIDENT AND EXECUTIVE DIRECTOR	Dianne Mooney
DIRECTOR OF BRAND MANAGEMENT	Gary Wright
RESEARCH MANAGER	Jon Williams

Oxmoor House, Inc.

EDITOR IN CHIEF	Nancy Fitzpatrick Wyatt
EXECUTIVE EDITOR	Susan Carlisle Payne
COPY CHIEF	Allison Long Lowery
EDITORS	Susan Ray, McCharen Pratt
DESIGNER	Melissa Clark
COPY EDITOR	Diane Rose
EDITORIAL ASSISTANTS	Julie Boston
TEST KITCHENS DIRECTOR	Elizabeth Tyler Austin
ASSISTANT TEST KITCHENS DIRECTOR	Julie Christopher
FOOD STYLIST	Kelley Self Wilton
TEST KITCHENS PROFESSIONALS	Kathleen Royal Phillips, Catherine Crowel Steele, Ashley T. Strickland
PHOTOGRAPHY DIRECTOR	Jim Bathie
SENIOR PHOTOGRAPHERS	Becky Luigart-Stayner, Randy Manor, Charles Walton IV
PHOTOGRAPHERS	Tina Cornett, William Dickey, Beth Dreiling, Brit Huckabay
CONTRIBUTING PHOTOGRAPHER	Howard Lee Puckett
SENIOR PHOTO STYLISTS	Cindy Barr, Kay Clarke, Lydia DeGaris-Pursell, Buffy Hargett
PHOTO STYLISTS	Melanie J. Clarke, Jan Guatro
ASSISTANT PHOTO STYLIST	Cari South
CONTRIBUTING PHOTO STYLIST	Leslie Byars Simpson
DIRECTOR OF PRODUCTION	Laura Lockhart
SENIOR PRODUCTION MANAGER	Greg Amason
PRODUCTION MANAGER	Tamara Nall
PRODUCTION ASSISTANT	Faye Porter Bonner
CONTRIBUTING COPY EDITOR	Lucas Whittington
EDITORIAL INTERN	Jill Baughman

Food just tastes better when it's grilled.

And best of all, in the South, you can fire up the grill just about any time of the year. All over the country, great gatherings are heralded by the sizzle of good food hitting that hot cooking grate. Gathering family and friends around the grill sets the stage for casual, comfortable occasions.

Whether you're a veteran grillmaster or a first-timer, we hope this collection of recipes will inspire you. It runs the gamut of grilled cuisine—from the classic American hamburger to finer culinary creations, such as planked tenderloin. All the recipes deliver on both taste and convenience, and we've made sure the presentation is helpful to cooks of all skill levels. We've indicated the proper heat level and cooking method, prep and cook times, and meat temperatures for each dish. Step-by-step instructions ensure perfect results every time. So get started now grilling some of our personal favorites:

- **Big Juicy Burgers** (page 40) are sure to be your new cookout staple.
- **Flank Steak with Dijon Vinaigrette** (page 47) is as versatile as it is delicious.
- **Smoky Chipotle Baby Back Ribs** (page 78) are the most mouthwatering barbecue ribs you'll ever eat; our expert tips let you grill them with ease.
- **Grilled Pound Cake with Peach Sauce** (page 102) will thrill you, as will the other desserts you cook on the grill.

In addition to all the delicious recipes, *Everyday Grilling* offers plenty of expertise to enhance your grilling experience:

- **Get back to basics.** We share the secrets to grilling success and introduce you to simple, surefire methods that produce astounding results.
- **Entertain with ease.** Don't spend your party working in the kitchen. Our on-the-grill menus and time-saving tips allow you to relax and join in the fun.
- **Get creative.** Move beyond our menus and create your own using the more than 120 recipes in our Mix-and-Match Cookbook beginning on page 56.

With these handy tips, secrets, and recipes at your fingertips, you'll grill with confidence and ease. So relax, keep it simple, and get that grill glowing!

contents

From simple weeknight suppers to casual gatherings of friends and family, we've collected the best tips, menus, and recipes for the most delicious meals ever. Find your best grill inspirations within these pages.

Mango Margarita, page 62

Grilled Corn with Jalapeño-Lime Butter, page 96

Mix-and-Match Cookbook

Ginger Grilled Pineapple with Ice Cream, page 104

Asian Chicken Wings, page 55

grilling: what you need to know

If you're looking for a cooking tool that's easy to use and maintain and adds incredible layers of flavor to any food—then get out of the kitchen and look in your backyard. In the next few pages, find tried-and-true tips about safety, choosing gadgets and grills, and finessing the fire—the key to grilling success.

No matter what your skill level, you can transform simple ingredients into mouthwatering meals. We hope this easy guide adds to your joy of grilling with family and friends.

Comparing Gas & Charcoal Grills

Charcoal or gas? It's a heated debate with die-hard fans in both camps. Consider the following points when choosing grills. Once you've decided what type of grill you want, use this guide to help you choose which features you'll need. If you're serious about your barbecue, go for both a charcoal and a gas grill.

Charcoal Grill

Some avid grillers think there's no substitute for building a fire with charcoal and tending the fire during the cooking process. Consider these features when choosing a charcoal grill.

• **Construction:** Look for a grill made of high-grade steel. A baked-on porcelain-enamel finish is more durable than a sprayed-on paint finish. Parts that are preassembled and/or welded provide strength.

• **Basic Features:** The grates on charcoal grills are either stainless steel or nickel plated, which makes them easy to clean and rust resistant. Wooden or plastic handles stay cool. Choose a grill that is large enough to cook with both direct and indirect heat— you need to be able to build a fire on opposite sides of the charcoal grate, leaving a space in the middle with no fire.

• **Added Conveniences:** A hinged food grate facilitates adding more charcoal when necessary. Grills with a thermometer help you regulate the grill's cooking internal temperature.

• **Advantages:** Grills are inexpensive and portable, and charcoal gives food an authentic smoky flavor.

• **Disadvantages:** Coals can be difficult to light, and it will take a while for them to warm up; heat can be tricky to regulate. Cleanup is not as easy as with gas.

Gas Grill

Gas grills give you greater control over heat, and they are much easier to light than charcoal grills. Here are some different points to ponder when you are selecting a gas grill.

• **Construction:** Select a gas grill made of high-grade steel with a baked-on finish. For a strong and stable grill, the cart should have welded legs.

• **Basic Features:** A basic gas grill has a food grate; burners for heat; and angled metal bars, lava rocks, or ceramic briquettes to distribute the heat. For the best heat control, purchase a grill that has two or more separate burners and angled metal bars over the burners. A lava rock system tends to collect grease, which can cause flare-ups.

• **Added Conveniences:** Gas gives you greater control over the heat and is easier to light than charcoal. Side burners, an option on some grills, make it easy to cook sauces and veggies along with

the meat. Many models also have convenient tables and condiment holders on the side.

• **Advantages:** Easily started with a push-button or rotary igniter. Optional accessories include smokers, steamers, and electric rotisseries. Cleanup is simple.

• **Disadvantages:** Significantly more expensive than charcoal grills. Food cooked on a gas grill doesn't have the smoky intensity or charcoal-grilled flavor.

Tending the Fire

Choosing between direct and indirect heat is simple: The greatest difference is that direct heat works best on foods that cook quickly, 20 to 30 minutes or less. If something needs to cook more than 30 minutes, use indirect heat.

Direct Heat

With direct-heat grilling, food cooks directly over the heat source. Quick-cooking foods suitable for direct heat include burgers, steaks, chops, chicken pieces, fish fillets, and veggies. To ensure even cooking, turn the foods only once. Direct heat is also used to sear meat and to get appealing grill marks.

Direct-Heat Cooking with a Charcoal Grill

• Distribute the hot coals evenly over the charcoal grate. Place the food grate over the coals, close the grill lid, and let the grate heat for 10 minutes.
• Place food on the food grate. Close the grill lid, lifting it only to turn the food or to test it for doneness.

Direct-Heat Cooking with a Gas Grill

• Turn all burners on High, close the grill lid, and preheat for 10 minutes.
• Adjust the burners to the temperature recommended in the recipe. Place food on the food grate. Close the grill lid, lifting it only to turn food or to check for doneness.

Indirect Heat

Indirect-heat grilling means the heat source is off to one side of the grill. This allows the heat to circulate around the food and cook it slowly and evenly. Foods that are fit for indirect heat include roasts, ribs, whole chickens, turkeys, and other large cuts of poultry or meat.

Indirect-Heat Cooking with a Charcoal Grill

• Evenly distribute the hot coals on opposite sides of the charcoal grate. Center a drip pan between the coals to catch drippings. Add water to the pan for longer cooking times to keep the drippings from burning.
• Place the food grate over the coals, close the grill lid, and let the grate heat for 10 minutes.
• Place food on the food grate. Close the grill lid, lifting it only to turn the food or to test for doneness.

Indirect-Heat Cooking with a Gas Grill

• Turn all burners on High, close the grill lid, and preheat for 10 minutes.
• Adjust the outside burners to the temperature recommended in the recipe. Place food on the food grate, and turn off the burners directly beneath the food. Close the grill lid, lifting it only to turn the food or to test for doneness.

a "hands-on" technique for determining the heat

A grill thermometer gives the most accurate measurement of how hot a fire is; the problem is it gives an accurate reading only when the grill is covered. If you don't have a covered grill, try this "hands-on" technique that allows you to estimate coal temperature by how long you can hold your hands above the coals at cooking level. A hot fire—which is between 400° and 500°, with coals that are barely covered with ash—allows a 2-second hand count. A medium fire—which is between 300° and 350°, with coals that are glowing through the gray ash—allows a 4-second hand count. A low fire—which is under 300°, with coals that are covered with a thick layer of ash—allows a 5-second hand count.

Cooking with Smoke and the Rotisserie

Once you become a pro grilling directly and indirectly, you might want to tackle some advanced techniques, namely smoke cooking and rotisserie cooking. Check the owner's manual for your grill for specific instructions for each method before you get started.

Evoke the very nature of the grill with the enticing aroma and flavor of smoked foods. A few chunks of wood added to your grill will let you almost taste the fire in these dishes . Once you get the hang of it, you'll start picking up on the nuances of flavor offered by different woods. (See pages 68 and 85.)

A rotisserie slowly rotates food impaled on a spit over a heat source. This allows heat to circulate evenly around meat or poultry while it self-bastes with its own juices. Rotisserie cooking uses a meat's natural juices to baste, rather than allowing those juices to drip into the flames. This results in meats that are exceptionally succulent and have an enticing crispy skin. Whether you use a charcoal or gas grill, you'll need a rotisserie attachment, which is easy to use and reduces your involvement to setting the timer.

Great Gadgets

Before you fire up the grill, assembling the proper equipment will help you cook up maximum flavor from your food with minimal effort. Here are some tools you'll want to have on hand.

• **Chimney Starter:** Every charcoal grill owner should have one of these. Place charcoal in the top. Wad newspaper in the bottom of the starter, place the chimney on the food grate or a fireproof surface, and ignite. When the coals are ready, pour them into the grill.

• **Butane Lighter:** No more looking for matches. A butane lighter has a long handle, which makes it safer and easier to use than matches—and it's easier to find!

• **Meat Thermometer:** Repeatedly checking the temperature of any meat can cool the pit and tack on extra cooking time. A digital roasting thermometer with probe can stay in the meat during cooking, allowing the grill lid to remain closed.

• **Timer:** A standard kitchen timer paired with a meat thermometer helps you turn out perfectly grilled food every time.

• **Skewers:** Placing small foods on skewers makes cooking easy. Soak wooden or bamboo skewers in water for 30 minutes before using them to prevent burning.

• **Metal Spatula:** A long-handled spatula with a stainless-steel blade is an essential grilling tool. Choose a wide spatula for easy turning.

• **Long-Handled Fork:** To lift large roasts and whole poultry from the grill after cooking, use a meat fork. To avoid losing flavorful juices, don't pierce meat during cooking.

• **Grill Tongs:** These are useful for turning most foods. Look for tongs with long handles and a spring hinge.

• **Basting Mop:** A good basting mop offers an efficient way to mop meats with sauces without keeping the grill lid open for long periods.

• **Basting Brush:** Use a basting brush to apply thick sauces to meats. Most labeled as "barbecue brushes" are for small jobs. For big jobs, look for a large paintbrush with natural bristles; synthetic bristles can melt if they touch a hot grate.

• **Barbecue Gloves:** Flame-retardant gloves protect your hands when working with hot grills and coals.

• **Grill Brush:** A stiff wire brush makes cleanup fast. Scrub down food grates before the smoker cools.

safety first

Using proper precautions ensures a carefree cookout.

Grilling Safety

• Always position the grill at least 10 feet away from your house, garage, or any flammable materials. Never grill indoors or under an awning or covered patio.
• Be sure to open the lid before lighting a gas grill.
• Store propane tanks outside, sheltered from direct sunlight.
• Never add lighter fluid to a fire already lit.
• Never use a grill that is not sturdy.
• Never use cooking sprays around a lit grill.
• Use barbecue gloves and long-handled grilling tools. Avoid wearing loose clothing when cooking out.
• Be mindful of children and pets around hot grills. Keep them away from a hot grill at all times.

Food Safety:

• After handling meat or before starting any meal preparations, it's important to scrub your hands with warm soapy water.
• Always defrost meat, fish, and poultry in the refrigerator, not at room temperature.
• Be sure not to use the same platter for cooked food that you used for raw food.
• If you intend to use a sauce for basting the food on the grill but you also want to serve the sauce at the table, reserve part of the sauce for basting and the other for the table. Never use a marinade as a baste or sauce after it has touched raw meat, fish, or poultry without vigorously boiling the marinade for 1 minute.

effortless entertaining

Treat your friends to carefree summer party menus and ideas.

one great grilled dinner

Here's an all-purpose menu you'll use time and again. Former corporate chef for the Minnesota Vikings, John Kirkpatrick knows how to please a crowd. His versatile dinner for friends is actually two flexible menus with interchangeable entrées. With John's make-ahead secrets you can show off your seemingly effortless grill mastery and enjoy the company of your guests.

menu

Serves 6

Teo's Punch

Bruschetta Gorgonzola and Apples

Hoisin and Bourbon-Glazed Pork Tenderloin with Three-Fruit Salsa

or Hoisin and Bourbon-Glazed Tuna with Tomato Relish

Rosemary-Roasted Mashed Potatoes

Giardiniera

Grasshopper Ice Cream Pie

Teo's Punch

Teo's Punch

Prep: 15 min.

Add some rum to this simple punch.

2 cups apple juice
2 (6-ounce) cans pineapple juice
1 (12-ounce) can cranberry juice concentrate, thawed and undiluted
1 (6-ounce) can orange juice concentrate, thawed and undiluted
1 (1-liter) bottle club soda, chilled

1. Combine first 4 ingredients; stir until blended. Add soda just before serving. Serve over ice. Yield: 10 cups.

Bruschetta Gorgonzola and Apples

Bruschetta Gorgonzola and Apples

DIRECT • MEDIUM
Prep: 12 min. • Cook: 2 min.

For this classic Italian appetizer, we chose Gorgonzola for its sweet creaminess, but any quality blue cheese will do. A slice of tart apple is a nice foil to the garlic and cheese.

$^1/_3$ **cup (about 1$^1/_2$ ounces)**
    crumbled Gorgonzola cheese
2 tablespoons butter, softened
1 tablespoon brandy or cognac
$^1/_8$ **teaspoon black pepper**
12 (1-ounce) slices diagonally cut
    French bread (about 1 inch thick)
Vegetable cooking spray
6 garlic cloves, halved
3 Granny Smith apples, each cut
    into 8 wedges

1. Combine first 4 ingredients in a small bowl, stirring until blended.
2. Lightly spray bread slices on both sides with cooking spray; grill bread slices over *Direct Medium* heat 30 to 60 seconds on each side or until lightly browned. Remove from grill. Rub cut sides of garlic over 1 side of each bread slice. Spread 2 teaspoons cheese mixture over each bread slice. Serve with apple wedges. Yield: 12 bruschetta.

make-ahead plan

Day before:
• Trim and butterfly pork.
• Prepare Giardiniera.
• Prepare Gorgonzola spread.
• Prepare Grasshopper Ice Cream Pie.

Morning of:
• Buy tuna.
• Ice beer.
• Mix hoisin sauce.
• Prepare Teo's punch without soda; chill.
• Chop vegetables for Tomato Relish or fruit for Three-Fruit Salsa.

Two hours ahead:
• Set up buffet area or dinner table.

One hour ahead:
• Assemble Tomato Relish or Three-Fruit Salsa.
• Cut up potatoes; preheat oven for potatoes.

45 minutes ahead:
• Prepare and preheat grill.
• Roast potatoes.
• Soak wood chips.

15 minutes ahead:
• Check grill; add additional charcoal as needed.
• Grill bread and slice apples for appetizer.
• Finish potatoes; keep warm.
• Add soda to punch.

As guests arrive:
• Add wood chips to grill.
• Prepare entrée.
• Set pie in refrigerator.
• Sit back and relax; you're all done except for the eating.

Hoisin and Bourbon-Glazed Tuna with Tomato Relish

Hoisin and Bourbon-Glazed Pork Tenderloin

Hoisin and Bourbon-Glazed Pork Tenderloin with Three-Fruit Salsa

DIRECT • MEDIUM-HIGH
Prep: 10 min. • Cook: 15 min. • Other: 35 min.

The basting sauce in this recipe is especially good because it has a range of flavors—sweet, sour, salty, woody, and spicy. Because the pork is butterflied, it picks up more of those flavors and cooks quickly.

¹/₃ **cup hoisin sauce**
2 tablespoons seasoned rice vinegar
2 tablespoons bourbon
2 tablespoons maple syrup
1¹/₂ teaspoons grated peeled fresh ginger
1¹/₂ teaspoons fresh lime juice
¹/₂ teaspoon chili paste with garlic
1 garlic clove, minced
2 (1-pound) pork tenderloins, trimmed
¹/₂ teaspoon salt
¹/₂ teaspoon freshly ground black pepper
1 cup hickory wood chips, soaked in water for at least 30 minutes
Three-Fruit Salsa

1. Combine first 8 ingredients in a small bowl; stir with a whisk.
2. Slice pork lengthwise, cutting to, but not through, other side. Open halves, laying pork flat.

Sprinkle pork with salt and pepper. Follow the grill's instructions for using wood chips. Grill pork over *Direct Medium-High* heat 5 minutes.
3. Turn and baste pork with hoisin mixture; grill 5 minutes. Turn and baste pork with hoisin mixture; grill 5 minutes or until pork is fully cooked and the internal temperature reaches 160°F. Let stand 5 minutes; cut pork into ½-inch slices. Serve with Three-Fruit Salsa. Yield: 8 servings.

Hoisin and Bourbon-Glazed Tuna with Tomato Relish

Follow step 1 at left. Sprinkle 6 (1-inch-thick) tuna steaks with ¼ teaspoon salt and ⅛ teaspoon freshly ground black pepper. Follow the grill's instructions for using wood chips. Baste tuna with the hoisin mixture; grill over *Direct Medium-High* heat 5 minutes. Turn and baste tuna with hoisin mixture; grill 5 minutes or until tuna just begins to flake easily with a fork. Serve with Tomato Relish. Yield: 6 servings.

Three-Fruit Salsa

Prep: 20 min.

This salsa takes on a tropical appeal with its Thai-inspired notes.

1 cup finely chopped peeled cantaloupe
1 cup finely chopped peeled mango
1 cup sliced small strawberries
¹/₂ cup finely chopped seeded peeled cucumber
¹/₂ cup finely chopped green bell pepper
¹/₂ cup finely chopped red onion
1¹/₂ tablespoons chopped fresh mint
1 tablespoon chopped fresh basil
2 tablespoons fresh lime juice
2 tablespoons finely chopped seeded jalapeño pepper
1 tablespoon honey
¹/₄ teaspoon salt

1. Stir together all ingredients in a bowl. Serve with a slotted spoon. Yield: 6 servings.

Tomato Relish

Prep: 20 min.

Cucumbers and mint enhance this easy relish, which will be as familiar as salsa.

2 cups chopped tomato
1 cup chopped yellow tomato
¹/₂ cup finely chopped seeded peeled cucumber
¹/₂ cup finely chopped green bell pepper
¹/₂ cup finely chopped red onion
3 tablespoons chopped fresh basil
2 tablespoons fresh lime juice
1¹/₂ teaspoons chopped fresh mint
¹/₂ teaspoon salt
¹/₂ teaspoon sugar
¹/₂ teaspoon dried crushed red pepper

1. Stir together all ingredients in a bowl. Serve with a slotted spoon. Yield: 6 servings.

salsa secrets

These tips will help you create the perfect salsa every time.

- Always use fresh, ripe ingredients.
- Use a very sharp knife for a clean chop.
- Be sure to include an ingredient that has a crunchy texture.
- Experiment until you get just the right combination of flavors and colors.
- Always taste the salsa and balance the "fire" before serving.

Rosemary-Roasted Mashed Potatoes

Prep: 10 min. • Cook: 30 min.

Roasting the potatoes for these mashers creates full-bodied flavor. If the appetizer course runs long, just stir in a little hot water to revive the creamy texture; the seasonings will remain just as robust.

2 pounds baking potatoes, cut into 1-inch pieces
1 tablespoon olive oil
$^1/_2$ teaspoon fresh or dried rosemary
$^1/_2$ teaspoon salt
$^1/_2$ teaspoon freshly ground black pepper
$^3/_4$ cup hot milk
$^1/_4$ cup chopped green onions
$^1/_4$ cup grated fresh Parmesan cheese
$^1/_4$ teaspoon garlic powder
1 (8-ounce) container sour cream

1. Combine first 5 ingredients in a lightly greased shallow pan; toss well to coat. Bake, uncovered, at 425°F for 30 minutes or until tender.
2. Combine milk and next 4 ingredients in a large bowl; add potato mixture. Mash with a potato masher to desired consistency. Serve immediately. Yield: 6 servings.

> Make sure the potatoes are arranged in a single layer and have enough room in the pan when roasting.

Giardiniera

Prep: 10 min. • Cook: 3 min. • Other: 8 hrs.

Giardiniera is great to prepare ahead and have on hand for a fabulous vegetable side or a quick snack.

$1^1/_2$ cups cider vinegar
$^1/_2$ cup water
2 tablespoons sugar
1 tablespoon salt
1 teaspoon black peppercorns
$^1/_2$ teaspoon mustard seeds
$^1/_2$ teaspoon dried dill weed
2 bay leaves
$^1/_2$ pound green beans, trimmed (about 8 ounces)
2 cups small cauliflower florets
2 cups (3-inch) diagonally cut asparagus
1 cup ($^1/_4$-inch) diagonally cut carrot
1 cup red bell pepper strips
6 green onion bottoms, trimmed
4 garlic cloves, halved

1. Combine first 8 ingredients in a large Dutch oven. Bring to a boil, reduce heat, and simmer 3 minutes.
2. Arrange green beans and next 6 ingredients in a large zip-top freezer bag. Carefully pour vinegar mixture over cauliflower mixture. Seal bag, and refrigerate 8 hours or overnight, turning occasionally. Remove vegetables from bag with a slotted spoon. Discard bay leaves. Yield: 6 servings.

Giardiniera

soft & easy

If your ice cream comes out of the freezer rock hard, here are some tips.

- To soften ice cream to make this recipe, let it stand at room temperature for about 30 minutes.
- Use a large bowl and a wooden spoon to stir ingredients into store-bought ice cream. A stand mixer also does the trick.
- You'll find slicing this pie a little easier if you let it soften a little in the refrigerator before slicing.

Grasshopper Ice Cream Pie

Prep: 10 min. • Cook: 1 min. • Other: 6 hrs.

This deceptively rich dessert offers a refreshing minty contrast to dinner.

1 cup chocolate wafer crumbs (about 20 cookies, such as Nabisco® Famous Chocolate Wafers)
2 tablespoons butter, melted
2 tablespoons milk
1 (7-ounce) jar marshmallow cream
¹/₄ cup green crème de menthe
2 tablespoons white crème de cacao
1 (8-ounce) container frozen whipped topping, thawed
3 cups vanilla ice cream, softened
1 tablespoon chocolate syrup

1. Combine crumbs and butter in a small bowl; stir with a fork until moist. Press into bottom of an ungreased 9-inch springform pan. Chill.

2. Combine milk and marshmallow cream in a microwave-safe bowl; microwave at HIGH 1 minute, stirring once. Add crème de menthe, crème de cacao, and whipped topping, stirring until blended.

3. Spread ice cream into prepared pan; top with marshmallow mixture. Cover and freeze at least 6 hours. Drizzle with chocolate syrup before serving. Yield: 12 servings.

a grillmaster's best recipes

Combine an Italian heritage with a Key West lifestyle and a passion for all things grilled, and you've got one grillmaster extraordinaire—Joe Famularo. To add zing to his grilled recipes, Famularo uses a combination of sauces, marinades, and herb rubs. These can be made in advance, leaving extra time for entertaining. Think Mediterranean-style celebrations on the patio, and you've got a taste of what Famularo is all about.

Mutton Snapper with Italian Flavors

Portobello Mushrooms with Mascarpone

Asparagus with Onion-and-Orange Vinaigrette

Cookbook authors Joe Famularo and Jean Carper

Sautéed Scallops on Lasagna Squares with Chili-Cream Sauce

Prep: 15 min. • Cook: 25 min.

Fresh pasta can be purchased in sheets at specialty food shops and cut into squares. Dry lasagna noodles can be substituted and cut into squares after cooking.

16 (4- x 4-inch) fresh lasagna squares
1½ pounds sea scallops
2½ tablespoons all-purpose flour, divided
1 tablespoon butter, divided
2 teaspoons canola oil, divided
1 teaspoon prepared chili powder
½ teaspoon curry powder
¾ cup low-fat milk
Pinch of salt
¼ cup thinly sliced green onions
Soy sauce

1. Cook lasagna squares according to package directions; drain. Cover with plastic wrap, and keep warm.

2. Dredge scallops in 2 tablespoons flour.

3. Heat 1½ teaspoons butter and 1 teaspoon oil in a large skillet over medium-high heat 2 minutes. Add half of the scallops, and cook about 2 minutes on each side or until lightly browned. Remove scallops, and set aside. Repeat procedure with remaining butter, oil, and scallops. Remove scallops, and set aside, reserving drippings in skillet.

4. Whisk remaining ½ tablespoon flour, chili powder, and curry powder into drippings in skillet. Cook over medium heat, whisking constantly, 1 minute. Gradually whisk in milk. Continue cooking over medium heat, whisking constantly, until thickened and bubbly. Stir in salt and scallops, and cook 1 minute or until thoroughly heated. Place 2 lasagna squares on individual plates; spoon scallops and sauce evenly over squares. Sprinkle each serving with green onions and a dash of soy sauce. Yield: 8 appetizer servings.

menu

Serves 8

Sautéed Scallops on Lasagna Squares with Chili-Cream Sauce

Spicy Gingered Shrimp

Mutton Snapper with Italian Flavors

Portobello Mushrooms with Mascarpone

Corn on the Cob with Chive-Fennel Butter

Asparagus with Onion-and-Orange Vinaigrette

Pineapple Slices with Honeydew Sauce

Sautéed Scallops on Lasagna Squares with Chili-Cream Sauce

Spicy Gingered Shrimp

DIRECT • HIGH

Prep: 25 min. • Cook: 4 min. • Other: 1 hr.

With only one shrimp per skewer, this appetizer is easy for guests to enjoy.

16 (12-inch) wooden skewers
16 unpeeled, large fresh shrimp
¹/₄ cup rice vinegar
¹/₄ cup frozen orange juice or lemonade concentrate, thawed
¹/₄ cup diced onion
1 tablespoon grated fresh ginger
¹/₂ teaspoon dried crushed red pepper

1. Soak skewers in water 30 minutes.
2. Peel shrimp, leaving tails on; devein shrimp, if desired. Place shrimp in a zip-top freezer bag.
3. Process rice vinegar and next 4 ingredients in a blender or food processor until smooth. Pour ¹/₃ cup marinade over shrimp; seal bag, and chill 30 minutes. Reserve remaining marinade.
4. Remove shrimp from marinade, discarding marinade in the bag. Thread 1 shrimp onto each skewer.
5. Grill over *Direct High* heat 2 minutes on each side, basting with reserved marinade. Serve immediately. Yield: 8 appetizer servings.

Mutton Snapper with Italian Flavors

DIRECT • HIGH

Prep: 15 min. • Cook: 30 min. • Other: 30 min.

2 (3-pound) whole mutton snapper, dressed
1 cup fresh lemon juice
¹/₄ cup chopped fresh basil
¹/₄ cup chopped fresh Italian parsley
¹/₄ cup chopped fresh oregano
¹/₄ cup minced onion
¹/₄ cup olive oil
4 large garlic cloves, minced
¹/₂ teaspoon salt
¹/₂ teaspoon freshly ground pepper
Garnishes: Italian parsley, oregano, lemon wedges

1. Make 2 (¹/₂-inch-deep) diagonal cuts on each side of fish. Arrange fish in a large shallow dish.
2. Combine lemon juice and next 8 ingredients. Set aside half of mixture to serve as a sauce with fish.
3. Brush inside of each fish with 1 tablespoon of lemon mixture. Pour remaining mixture over fish. Cover and chill 30 minutes, turning fish once.
4. Remove fish from marinade, and reserve the marinade. Pour the marinade into a small saucepan, bring to a boil, and boil for 1 full minute. Place fish in 2 lightly greased grill baskets.
5. Grill over *Direct High* heat about 15 minutes on each side or until fish just begins to flake with a fork, basting often with boiled marinade. Garnish, if desired. Serve immediately with reserved sauce. Yield: 8 servings.

Portobello Mushrooms with Mascarpone

DIRECT • MEDIUM

Prep: 15 min. • Cook: 14 min.

Most often used as a dessert cheese, mascarpone provides a mild complement to these herby portobellos.

8 large fresh portobello mushroom caps
Vegetable cooking spray
1¹/₂ tablespoons fresh lemon juice
2 garlic cloves, minced
1 tablespoon minced fresh basil
1 tablespoon minced fresh oregano
¹/₄ teaspoon freshly ground pepper
¹/₃ cup chicken broth
¹/₂ cup (4 ounces) mascarpone cheese
Garnish: fresh basil sprig

1. Coat mushrooms with cooking spray; set aside.
2. Stir together lemon juice and garlic in a small saucepan; cook over medium heat 1 to 2 minutes. Stir in basil and next 3 ingredients; bring to a boil. Remove from heat.
3. Brush mushrooms with herb mixture, applying generously to the underside. Divide mascarpone into 8 portions, and roll into balls.
4. Grill mushrooms, top side up, over *Direct Medium* heat 5 to 7 minutes. Turn mushrooms; top each mushroom with a cheese ball. Grill 5 to 7 minutes. Garnish, if desired. Serve immediately. Yield: 8 servings.

Spicy Gingered Shrimp

Corn on the Cob with Chive-Fennel Butter

DIRECT • MEDIUM
Prep: 20 min. • Cook: 30 min. • Other: 30 min.

8 ears fresh corn with husks
2 tablespoons butter, melted
2 large garlic cloves, minced
2 teaspoons fresh chives, minced
¹/₄ teaspoon fennel seeds

1. Soak corn in cold water for at least 30 minutes. Pull back husks on each ear of corn, leaving them attached at the stem; remove and discard the corn silks.
2. Stir together butter and next 3 ingredients; brush onto each ear. Pull husks back over corn. Tie wet string around husks, if desired.
3. Grill over *Direct Medium* heat 25 to 30 minutes, turning 3 or 4 times. Don't worry if the husks brown or burn. Remove from grill; when cool enough to handle, carefully pull husks back and cut them off with a knife. Serve corn warm. Yield: 8 servings.

Corn on the Cob with Chive-Fennel Butter

Asparagus with Onion-and-Orange Vinaigrette

DIRECT • MEDIUM
Prep: 10 min. • Cook: 8 min.

2 pounds fresh asparagus
2 tablespoons olive oil
¹/₂ teaspoon salt
¹/₂ teaspoon freshly ground pepper
1 small celery heart with leaves, minced (about ¹/₄ cup)
¹/₄ cup minced red onion
1 tablespoon minced carrot
1 tablespoon minced fresh ginger
1 teaspoon grated orange zest
¹/₃ cup unsweetened apple juice
2 tablespoons rice vinegar
1 tablespoon honey

1. Snap off tough ends of asparagus. Brush asparagus with oil and season with salt and pepper.
2. Grill over *Direct Medium* heat 6 to 8 minutes, turning occasionally.
3. Stir together celery and next 7 ingredients; spoon over asparagus. Yield: 8 servings.

Pineapple Slices with Honeydew Sauce

DIRECT • MEDIUM
Prep: 15 min. • Cook: 10 min. • Other: 2 hrs.

To make measuring honey easier, give your ¹/₄ cup measure a quick spritz of cooking spray before pouring in the honey.

1 ripe honeydew melon, peeled, seeded, and cubed
¹/₄ cup honeydew melon liqueur
¹/₄ cup honey
1 pineapple, peeled and cored
1¹/₂ tablespoons chopped fresh mint
Garnishes: fresh mint sprigs, fresh raspberries

1. Process first 3 ingredients in a food processor until smooth, stopping to scrape down sides. Transfer to a bowl. Cover and chill 2 hours.
2. Cut pineapple in half lengthwise. Cut each half into 4 wedges.
3. Grill pineapple over *Direct Medium* heat about 5 minutes on each side or until lightly browned.
4. Pour honeydew mixture into 8 chilled bowls, sprinkle evenly with chopped mint. Arrange pineapple over honeydew mixture. Garnish, if desired. Serve immediately. Yield: 8 servings.

> Long spears of asparagus have a mild flavor and delicate texture that perk up nicely when matched with this tangy citrus vinaigrette.

poolside luau

Dive into good times with our exotic—but easy—celebration. Head poolside with an island-themed party full of tropical selections, all of which can be made ahead. All you have to do the day of the party is put on your sunglasses and grill the chicken.

Fruit Punch

Prep: 5 min.

If you don't drink alcohol, leave out the rum; the recipe tastes just as good without it.

3 cups cranberry juice cocktail
2 cups pineapple juice
2 cups orange juice
1 (1-liter) bottle ginger ale, chilled
3/4 to 1 cup light rum
Garnish: 1 star fruit, cut into
   1/4-inch slices

1. Combine first 3 ingredients in a large pitcher, and chill up to 8 hours, if desired. Stir ginger ale and rum into juice mixture just before serving. Serve over ice; garnish, if desired. Yield: 12 cups.

Macadamia-Mango Chicken

DIRECT • MEDIUM-HIGH
Prep: 10 min. • Cook: 12 min. • Other: 1 hr.

The colorful Mango Salsa that accompanies this chicken also pairs nicely with beef, fish, shrimp, or tortilla chips.

1/2 cup soy sauce
2 garlic cloves, minced
1 tablespoon light brown sugar
1 tablespoon olive oil
1 teaspoon grated fresh ginger
6 skinned and boned chicken
   breasts
Mustard Sauce
3 tablespoons macadamia nuts,
   chopped
Mango Salsa

1. Combine first 5 ingredients in a shallow dish or zip-top freezer bag; add chicken. Cover or seal, and chill 1 hour, turning once.
2. Remove chicken from marinade, discarding marinade.
3. Grill over *Direct Medium-High* heat 4 to 6 minutes on each side or until juices run clear and the internal temperature reaches 170°F. Drizzle with Mustard Sauce, and sprinkle evenly with nuts. Serve with Mango Salsa. Yield: 6 servings.

Mustard Sauce

Prep: 5 min.

1/2 cup Dijon mustard
2 tablespoons light brown sugar
2 tablespoons pineapple juice
1/8 to 1/4 teaspoon ground
   cayenne pepper

1. Stir together all ingredients; cover and chill up to 24 hours, if desired. Yield: 2/3 cup.

Mango Salsa

Prep: 10 min. • Other: 2 hrs.

2 ripe mangoes (about 1 pound),
   peeled and diced*
1 medium red bell pepper, diced
1 jalapeño pepper, seeded and
   diced
3 tablespoons chopped fresh
   cilantro
2 tablespoons chopped fresh mint
1 small red onion, chopped
2 tablespoons honey
1 tablespoon fresh lime juice
1/4 teaspoon ground cayenne
   pepper
1/4 teaspoon salt

1. Stir together all ingredients; cover and chill at least 2 hours. Yield: 2 cups.
*1 (26-ounce) jar refrigerated mango slices can be substituted.

make-ahead plan

Day before:
• Prepare Fruit Punch, and chill.
• Prepare Mustard Sauce and Mango Salsa for Macadamia-Mango Chicken, and chill.

• Prepare Peanut-Noodle Salad, and chill.
• Prepare Tropical Fruit Salad, and chill.
• Prepare Banana-Coconut Ice Cream, and freeze.

One hour ahead:
• Marinate and grill chicken.
• Prepare Frozen Coffee Cooler.

Fruit Punch

Tropical Fruit Salad

Peanut-Noodle
Salad

Macadamia-Mango
Chicken

Peanut-Noodle Salad

Peanut-Noodle Salad

Prep: 25 min.

This recipe can be easily halved for a weeknight side dish. Serve chilled or at room temperature.

2 large cucumbers
1 cup soy sauce
¹/₂ cup coconut milk
¹/₂ cup rice wine vinegar
¹/₂ cup chunky peanut butter
4 garlic cloves, minced
1 teaspoon sesame oil
¹/₂ to 1 teaspoon dried crushed
 red pepper
¹/₂ teaspoon salt
1 (16-ounce) package soba
 noodles or angel hair pasta,
 cooked
1 (8-ounce) package shredded
 fresh carrot
6 green onions, cut diagonally
 into 1¹/₂-inch pieces

1. Peel cucumbers; cut in half lengthwise, removing and discarding seeds. Cut cucumber halves into half-moon shaped slices.
2. Whisk together soy sauce and next 7 ingredients in a large bowl; add cucumber, pasta, carrot, and green onions, tossing to coat. Cover and chill up to 24 hours, if desired. Yield: 6 to 8 servings.

Tropical Fruit Salad

Prep: 30 min. • Other: 8 hrs.

Enjoy this fruit salad for breakfast, lunch, or dinner.

2 (20-ounce) cans pineapple
 chunks, undrained
3 tablespoons honey
1 teaspoon grated orange zest
1 teaspoon grated lime zest
¹/₂ cup fresh lime juice
6 medium oranges, peeled and
 sliced
4 kiwifruit, peeled, halved, and
 sliced
2 papayas, peeled and cubed*
Garnishes: sweetened flaked
 coconut, fresh mint leaves

1. Drain pineapple, reserving ¹/₂ cup juice.
2. Stir together reserved juice, honey, and next 3 ingredients in a large bowl; add pineapple, orange slices, and remaining fruit, tossing gently to coat. Cover and chill up to 24 hours. Garnish, if desired. Yield: 6 to 8 servings.
*2 mangoes, peeled and cubed, can be substituted for papayas.

Tropical Fruit Salad

Frozen Coffee Cooler

Frozen Coffee Cooler

Prep: 10 min.

This frosty, flavorful beverage hits the spot on a warm summer day.

6 cups ice cubes
4 cups brewed coffee, cooled
1 cup coffee liqueur
³/₄ cup sugar
1 teaspoon ground cinnamon
1 cup half-and-half or milk
Garnishes: whipped cream,
 ground cinnamon

1. Process half of first 5 ingredients in a blender until smooth. Pour coffee mixture into a large pitcher. Repeat with remaining half of first 5 ingredients, and pour into pitcher.
2. Stir half-and-half into coffee mixture, and garnish, if desired. Serve immediately. Yield: about 8 cups.

Banana-Coconut Ice Cream

Banana-Coconut Ice Cream

Prep: 30 min. • Cook: 30 min. • Other: 4 hrs.

Ripe bananas lend the richest flavor.

2 cups sweetened flaked coconut
1 cup sugar
6 egg yolks
4 cups milk
2 cups half-and-half
1 (15-ounce) can cream of coconut
2 teaspoons vanilla extract
3 ripe bananas, mashed
Garnish: toasted sweetened
**   flaked coconut**

1. Bake coconut in a shallow pan at 350°F, stirring occasionally, 10 minutes or until toasted.

2. Whisk together sugar, egg yolks, and milk in a heavy saucepan over medium heat; cook, whisking constantly, 20 minutes or until mixture thickens and will coat a spoon (do not boil).

3. Remove from heat; whisk in coconut, half-and-half, cream of coconut, and vanilla. Fold in banana. Cover and chill 3 hours.

4. Pour mixture into freezer container of a 1-gallon hand-turned or electric ice-cream freezer. Freeze according to manufacturer's instructions.

5. Pack freezer with additional ice and rock salt, and let stand 1 hour before serving. Garnish, if desired. Yield: 2½ quarts.

Use a vegetable peeler to quickly shave pretty garnishes of coconut curls from a piece of fresh coconut.

take it to the tropics

Island-Inspired Decorating Tips

- Buy tropical plants from your local garden center.
- Mix-and-match colorful dishes and serving pieces for an extra-special touch.
- Buy kiwifruit, coconuts, and other produce from the grocery store; place in straw or wicker baskets for a centerpiece.
- Create a natural look with bamboo or wooden chairs and tables.
- Purchase leis from a party store, or make your own from fresh flowers.
- Invite your guests to wear Hawaiian shirts or other tropical attire.

just grill...and chill

For the ultimate make-ahead opportunity, grill these recipes up to a day ahead, and then chill until you're ready to eat. Get that unbeatable grilled flavor for slow and easy summer gatherings even on weeknights.

Smoky Vegetable Guacamole

DIRECT • MEDIUM
Prep: 10 min. • Cook: 12 min.

Slather some of this spread on the bread the next time you make your favorite grilled chicken sandwich.

4 small avocados, peeled and
  seeded
3 tablespoons fresh lime juice
$^1/_2$ cup sour cream
2 tablespoons balsamic vinegar
$^1/_2$ teaspoon salt
1 large sweet onion, cut into
  $^3/_4$-inch-thick slices
6 large shallots, peeled
1 large red bell pepper, seeded
  and quartered
2 jalapeño peppers
2 tablespoons olive oil
Tortilla chips

1. Mash avocados and lime juice together in a medium bowl. Stir in sour cream, vinegar, and salt. Cover and chill.
2. Brush onion, shallots, bell pepper, and jalapeños with oil. Grill vegetables over *Direct Medium* heat until tender, turning once. The onion and shallots will take 10 to 12 minutes. The bell peppers will take 6 to 8 minutes. The jalapeños will take 2 to 3 minutes. Remove vegetables; cool.
3. Remove seeds from jalapeño peppers. Chop onion, shallots, bell pepper, and jalapeños; stir into avocado mixture. Cover and chill, if desired. Serve with tortilla chips. Yield: 4 cups.

Fisherman's Salad

DIRECT • HIGH
Prep: 10 min. • Cook: 10 min. • Other: 30 min.

2 pounds fish fillets (salmon,
  halibut, swordfish, grouper, or
  other firm fish), each about
  1 inch thick
2 tablespoons olive oil
$^3/_4$ teaspoon salt, divided
$^1/_2$ teaspoon freshly ground
  pepper, divided
$^2/_3$ cup mayonnaise
2 tablespoons fresh lemon juice
3 celery ribs, sliced
$^1/_4$ cup minced onion
1 (2-ounce) jar diced pimiento,
  drained
2 tablespoons chopped fresh
  parsley
2 tablespoons capers, drained
Leaf lettuce
Garnish: tomato wedges

1. Brush fillets with olive oil; sprinkle with ½ teaspoon salt and ¼ teaspoon pepper, and place in a lightly greased grill basket.
2. Grill over *Direct High* heat 8 to 10 minutes or until fish is just opaque at the center and slightly firm to the touch, turning once. Cool fish, and flake.
3. Stir together mayonnaise, lemon juice, and remaining ¼ teaspoon salt and ¼ teaspoon pepper in a large bowl; add fish, celery, and next 4 ingredients, tossing lightly. Cover and chill 30 minutes or up to 24 hours. Serve on lettuce-lined plates; garnish, if desired. Yield: 6 servings.

Grilled Marinated Vegetables

DIRECT • MEDIUM-HIGH
Prep: 15 min. • Cook: 15 min. • Other: 8½ hrs.

These veggies taste great if you want to serve them hot from the grill, but they develop even more flavor overnight.

$^1/_3$ cup white balsamic vinegar
2 tablespoons olive oil
2 shallots, finely chopped
1 teaspoon dried Italian
  seasoning
$^1/_4$ teaspoon salt
$^1/_4$ teaspoon pepper
$1^1/_2$ teaspoons molasses
$^1/_2$ pound carrots
1 large red bell pepper, seeded
1 large yellow bell pepper, seeded
2 large zucchini
2 large yellow squash
1 large onion

1. Combine first 7 ingredients in a large bowl. Set aside.
2. Cut carrots and remaining vegetables into large pieces. Add vegetables to vinegar mixture, tossing to coat. Let stand 30 minutes, stirring occasionally. Drain vegetables, reserving vinegar mixture. Arrange vegetables in a grill basket.
3. Grill over *Direct Medium-High* heat until crisp-tender 10 to 15 minutes, turning occasionally.
4. Return vegetables to reserved vinegar mixture, tossing gently. Cover and refrigerate at least 8 hours. Yield: 6 cups.

Grilled Marinated Vegetables

Amazing Taco Salad

DIRECT • MEDIUM-HIGH

Prep: 10 min. • Cook: 10 min. • Other: 10 min.

1 large red bell pepper

1 teaspoon prepared chili powder

$^1/_4$ teaspoon salt

$^1/_4$ teaspoon black pepper

4 (4-ounce) skinned and boned
   chicken breasts

1 (15-ounce) can black beans,
   rinsed and drained

$^1/_4$ cup finely chopped onion

$^1/_4$ cup Catalina dressing

$^1/_4$ cup chutney

4 cups shredded iceberg
lettuce

$^1/_2$ cup (2 ounces) shredded
   Cheddar cheese

Tortilla chips

1. Cut 4 sides lengthwise from red pepper. Discard stem and seeds. Combine chili powder, salt, and pepper; sprinkle evenly over chicken and pepper quarters.
2. Grill chicken and pepper quarters over *Direct Medium-High* heat 4 to 5 minutes on each side or until chicken is firm and juices run clear, and pepper is tender. Cool slightly; slice chicken and pepper into strips.
3. Combine chicken and pepper strips, beans, and next 3 ingredients; toss well. Cover and chill 10 minutes or until ready to serve.
4. To serve, place 1 cup lettuce on each of 4 serving plates. Arrange chicken mixture evenly over lettuce; sprinkle each serving with 2 tablespoons cheese. Arrange tortilla chips on each plate. Yield: 4 servings.

Italian Eggplant Vinaigrette

DIRECT • MEDIUM

Prep: 25 min. • Cook: 18 min. • Other: 9 hrs.

2 large eggplants

2$^1/_2$ teaspoons salt, divided

2 small zucchini

2 small yellow squash

$^1/_4$ cup olive oil

4 garlic cloves, minced

$^1/_4$ cup chopped fresh basil

$^1/_4$ cup chopped fresh mint

3 tablespoons balsamic
vinegar

Garnish: fresh basil sprigs

1. Cut eggplants crosswise into $^1/_2$-inch slices; sprinkle cut sides with 1$^1/_2$ teaspoons salt. Place in a single layer on paper towels; let stand 1 hour.

2. Cut zucchini and squash lengthwise into ¼-inch-thick slices; set aside.

3. Process ½ teaspoon salt, the olive oil, minced garlic, chopped basil, chopped mint, and balsamic vinegar in a food processor, stopping to scrape down sides.

4. Rinse eggplant slices with water, and pat dry. Brush slices with olive oil mixture; sprinkle with ¼ teaspoon salt. Arrange eggplant in a single layer on the cooking grate. Grill eggplant slices over *Direct Medium* heat 8 to 10 minutes or until lightly browned, turning and brushing with olive oil mixture. Remove eggplant from grill.

5. Sprinkle zucchini and squash slices with remaining ¼ teaspoon salt; brush with olive oil mixture. Arrange slices in a single layer on the cooking grate. Grill zucchini and squash slices over *Direct Medium* heat 6 to 8 minutes, turning once.

6. Arrange grilled eggplant, zucchini, and squash in an even layer in a 13- x 9-inch baking dish. Pour remaining olive oil mixture over vegetables. Cover and chill 8 hours. Garnish, if desired. Yield: 6 servings.

Grilled Potato Salad

DIRECT • MEDIUM-HIGH
Prep: 6 min. • Cook: 20 min.

1½ pounds small round red
   potatoes, quartered
1 small onion, thinly sliced
1 medium red bell pepper,
   cut into 1-inch-wide strips
1 medium green bell pepper,
   cut into 1-inch-wide strips
Vegetable cooking spray
4 bacon slices
¼ cup plus 2 tablespoons white
   vinegar
¼ cup plus 2 tablespoons
   chicken broth
2 tablespoons vegetable oil
1 teaspoon minced garlic (about
   2 cloves)

1. Place potatoes, onion, and pepper strips in a grill basket coated with cooking spray; coat vegetables with cooking spray. Place bacon slices over vegetables. Place grill basket on the cooking grate, bacon side up. Grill over *Direct Medium-High* heat 15 to 20 minutes or until vegetables are tender, turning once.

2. While vegetables cook, combine vinegar and next 3 ingredients in a jar; cover tightly, and shake vigorously. Set aside.

3. Place grilled vegetables in a large bowl; crumble bacon slices over vegetables. Shake vinegar dressing to mix, and pour over vegetables; toss well. Serve immediately, or cover and chill until ready to serve. Yield: 6 to 8 servings.

Grilled Vegetable Antipasto

DIRECT • MEDIUM
Prep: 10 min. • Cook: 30 min. • Other: 2 hrs.

Grilling the zucchini and the eggplant makes them more absorbent, which allows them to soak up more of the flavorful vinaigrette.

2 red bell peppers
2 zucchini, each cut in half
   lengthwise (about 1 pound)
2 Japanese eggplants, each cut in
   half lengthwise (about 8 ounces)
¼ cup chopped fresh parsley
¼ cup balsamic vinegar
1 tablespoon extra-virgin olive oil
¼ teaspoon salt
6 garlic cloves, peeled and
   crushed

1. Grill peppers over *Direct Medium* heat 15 to 20 minutes or until charred, turning peppers occasionally. Place peppers in a zip-top freezer bag; seal and let stand 15 minutes. Peel peppers; discard seeds and membranes. Coarsely chop peppers; return to zip-top freezer bag.

2. Grill zucchini and eggplant over *Direct Medium* heat about 10 minutes, turning occasionally.

Remove zucchini and eggplant from grill; coarsely chop zucchini and eggplant, and add to chopped peppers.

3. Combine parsley and next 4 ingredients, stirring with a whisk. Pour the parsley mixture over pepper mixture. Seal bag; squeeze bag gently to coat. Refrigerate at least 2 hours or overnight. Yield: 4 servings.

Grilled Chicken Salad with Cherries

DIRECT • MEDIUM-HIGH
Prep: 15 min. • Cook: 10 min.

6 (4-ounce) skinned and boned
   chicken breasts
¼ teaspoon salt
¼ teaspoon black pepper
2 teaspoons extra-virgin olive oil
⅓ cup water
¼ cup red wine vinegar
2 tablespoons minced shallots
1 tablespoon extra-virgin olive oil
2 teaspoons Dijon mustard
1½ teaspoons minced fresh or
   ½ teaspoon dried thyme
½ teaspoon sugar
¼ teaspoon salt
⅛ teaspoon black pepper
6 cups gourmet salad greens
1½ cups coarsely chopped
   pitted sweet cherries

1. Sprinkle chicken evenly with the salt and pepper. Brush or spray chicken with 2 teaspoons olive oil.

2. Grill the chicken over *Direct Medium-High* heat until the juices run clear and the meat is no longer pink in the center, 8 to 10 minutes, turning once. Cut into ¼-inch-thick slices.

3. To prepare vinaigrette, combine water and next 8 ingredients in a small bowl; stir with a whisk. Cover and chill chicken and vinaigrette until ready to serve.

4. Arrange salad greens on plates, and top with sliced chicken, chopped cherries, and vinaigrette. Yield: 6 servings.

vine advice

Gone are the hard-and-fast rules you've typically heard for pairing wine and food. These days wine experts share a few simple guidelines and then encourage experimentation with the myriad of flavors available. In reality, the best match for wine is good conversation.

With all the wine varieties available, it's easy to get overwhelmed and analyze each selection until your menu becomes a burden rather than a pleasure. However, you should also be wary of reducing your wine choices to the "white wine with white meat, red wine with red meat" concept. The way a food is prepared, rather than the food itself, is more important in determining the wine to be served.

Here's the simplest approach to food and wine pairing: When food and wines have similar flavors and characteristics (see chart on opposite page), they won't overpower each other. This is why you might serve a sweet Sauternes with dessert. To match the tart flavors of feta and garlic in Grilled Tomato Pizzas on page 91, an acidic wine such as Pinot Noir is a good choice.

You may prefer to choose a wine that contrasts with your food. Because alcohol accentuates heat, hot and spicy dishes (like Hickory-Grilled Jerk Chicken on page 81) are enhanced when served with a slightly sweet wine like a Riesling, due to its lower alcohol content. Serve a light, acidic wine such as Sauvignon Blanc with a rich food like Molasses-Grilled Chops with Horseradish Sauce on page 64.

Best Bets

The novice wine aficionado may want to start small. These six wines—three white and three red—will please even the most discriminating

palate and make a good match for most flavors. The white wines taste especially good with most grilled poultry, fish, and shellfish recipes; dare to go beyond just red meat with these red wines.

- **Chardonnay,** perhaps the most popular of all white wine grapes, has buttery, fruity, vanilla, and toasty flavors and is usually dry.

It pairs well with a host of entrées, especially grilled.
- **Sauvignon Blanc,** a dry white wine that's lighter in color and body and more citrusy and herbaceous than Chardonnay, is a food-friendly wine with an acidic zing.
- **Riesling** is a light, fruity wine with a floral fragrance and a slight

sweetness. It's a refreshing choice for spicy, salty, or smoked foods.

• **Cabernet Sauvignon** is a full-bodied and intense wine that possesses peppery, berry, and vanilla qualities that pair well with beef, poultry, pasta, and game meats.

• **Merlot,** with its hints of berry, black cherry, plum, spice, and tobacco, is a softer, more supple wine than Cabernet. It pairs well with poultry and lamb.

• **Pinot Noir** is more delicate than Cabernet or Merlot. Whispers of spicy cherries and earthy nuances create a complex flavor that pairs well with beef and ham.

Easy as 1, 2, 3

Once you find your footing and decide you want your wine mastery to match your prowess at the grill, here are three questions to ask when selecting a wine. As you consider these elements, remember that, ultimately, you want a wine with flavors you enjoy.

• What is the recipe's main ingredient? Are there any other flavoring agents? For example, is the dish salty or seasoned with herbs?

• How was the dish prepared? Was it grilled, smoked, or simmered for hours?

• What kinds of wines are available to you, and what fits your budget?

wine and food pairing chart

Food	Wine (Those listed by grape variety are in regular type; regional wines are in italic.)
Hot, spicy foods Ingredients like: chiles, ginger, and pepper Common cuisines: Chinese, Indian, Mexican, and Thai	**Slightly sweet, fruity, light wines** such as *Burgundy*, Chenin Blanc, Gamay Beaujolais, Gewürztraminer, Riesling, and white Zinfandels
Acidic, tart foods Ingredients like: feta cheese, garlic, lemon, tomatoes, vinegar, citrus Common cuisines: Creole, Greek, Italian, and Japanese	**High-acid wines** such as *Chianti*, Pinot Noir, Sauvignon Blanc, and sparkling whites
Rich foods Ingredients like: butter, cheese, lobster, red meats, and salmon Common cuisines: French, German, Italian, and Southern	**Acidic, citrus wine** such as Sauvignon Blanc **Oaky, toasty, buttery wine** such as Chardonnay **Tannic (tart), darker reds** like Cabernet Sauvignon, Merlot, and dark Zinfandel
Salty or smoked foods Ingredients like: olives, salt-cured or smoked meats, and soy sauce Common cuisines: Japanese, German, Greek, and Southern	**Slightly sweet, fruity, light wines** such as Chenin Blanc, Gamay Beaujolais, Gewürztraminer, Riesling, sparkling wine, and white Zinfandels
Sweet foods Ingredients like: coconut, corn, fruits, mint, and thyme Common cuisines: Chinese, French, Indian, and Thai	**For foods other than desserts:** slightly sweet wines such as Chenin Blanc, Riesling, and Gewürztraminer **For desserts:** sweet wines such as Madeira, Ruby Port, *Sauternes*, sherry, and sparkling wines such as Asti Spumante **Note:** Pair sweet foods with sweet wines, but the food should never be sweeter than the wine.

quick-and-easy family favorites

Savor simple suppers
for everyday meals and
special occasions.

father's day courtside cookout

Pamper Dad on his special day with a sports-themed cookout the whole family will enjoy.

menu

Serves 6

Spiced Iced Tea

Hickory-Smoked Kabobs

Dad's Braggin' Beans

Colorful Coleslaw

Championship Cookies

Win or lose, serve up these juicy grilled kabobs after a Father's Day sports outing. Take this menu courtside for a memorable family event. At home, prepare the tea and coleslaw and transport in a cooler. Bake the beans and bring them in a dish you can set on a corner of the grill to warm. Marinate the meat and assemble the kabobs. At the cookout, fire up your grill—cook the kabobs first and the cookies after dinner.

Spiced Iced Tea

Prep: 10 min. • Cook: 5 min. • Other: 5 min.

16 cups water
1 teaspoon cardamom seeds
1 teaspoon whole allspice
3 (3-inch) cinnamon sticks, halved
8 regular-size tea bags
3/4 cup sugar
Garnish: fresh mint sprigs

1. Bring first 4 ingredients to a boil in a Dutch oven; remove from heat, and add tea bags. Cover and steep 5 minutes. Pour mixture through a wire-mesh strainer into a large pitcher, discarding tea bags. Stir in sugar; chill. Serve over ice; garnish, if desired. Yield: 1 gallon.

Hickory-Smoked Kabobs

DIRECT • MEDIUM-HIGH

Prep: 15 min. • Cook: 10 min. • Other: 8 hrs.

1 1/2 pounds top sirloin steak, cut into 1 1/2-inch cubes
1 (8-ounce) bottle Russian dressing
1/4 cup Worcestershire sauce
2 teaspoons liquid smoke
1/2 teaspoon freshly ground pepper
3 small onions
12 large fresh mushrooms
1 large green bell pepper, cut into 1 1/2-inch pieces
1 large red bell pepper, cut into 1 1/2-inch pieces
3 lemons, cut into wedges
Additional lemon wedges (optional)

1. Place steak cubes in a shallow dish. Combine dressing and next 3 ingredients; stir well. Pour half of marinade over meat. Cover and marinate in refrigerator 8 hours; stir occasionally. Refrigerate remaining marinade to use for basting.

2. Cook onions 2 minutes in boiling water. Drain and cut onions into quarters.

3. Remove meat from marinade, discarding marinade in the dish. Alternate meat, onion quarters, mushrooms, pepper pieces, and lemon wedges on 6 (14-inch) metal skewers.

4. Grill kabobs over *Direct Medium-High* heat 4 minutes on each side or until the meat is medium-rare, basting frequently with reserved marinade. Squeeze additional lemon wedges over kabobs before serving, if desired. Yield: 6 servings.

Stuff tennis ball cans with flatware and sports towels; tie with new shoestrings. Use lids as coasters and wristbands for clever glass cozies.

Dad's Braggin' Beans

Colorful Coleslaw

Hickory-Smoked Kabobs

greatest

TO DAD

Dad's Braggin' Beans

Prep: 15 min. • **Cook:** 2 hrs.

$^{1}/_{2}$ **pound hot ground pork sausage**
1 **large Vidalia onion, chopped**
2 **(16-ounce) cans pork and beans, undrained**
1 **(15-ounce) can black beans, drained**
$^{1}/_{2}$ **cup firmly packed dark brown sugar**
$^{1}/_{2}$ **cup hickory-smoked barbecue sauce**
$^{1}/_{3}$ **cup ketchup**
$^{1}/_{4}$ **cup coarse-grained mustard**
$^{1}/_{4}$ **cup molasses**
1 **jalapeño pepper, minced**
1 **to 2 teaspoons prepared chili powder**
4 **bacon slices**

1. Cook sausage and onion in a skillet, stirring until sausage crumbles and is no longer pink. Drain. Combine sausage mixture, pork and beans, and next 8 ingredients in a shallow lightly greased $2^{1}/_{2}$-quart casserole; stir well. Place bacon slices on beans.
2. Bake, uncovered, at 350°F for $1^{1}/_{2}$ to 2 hours or until desired thickness. Yield: 6 servings.

These rustic, stick-to-your-ribs beans bake with sausage, brown sugar, and barbecue sauce to fully develop the flavors that make them cookout classics.

party options

Adapt this sporty theme to a variety of occasions, such as launching a new tennis league, hosting a sports-related birthday party, having a tennis team reunion, or arranging a Wimbledon cookout. Or change the honored sport to golf, softball, or volleyball, and have a cookout in the backyard.

Colorful Coleslaw

Prep: 10 min. • **Other:** 1 hr.

Carrot, red onion, and cilantro lend a burst of color to this coleslaw.

1 **small cabbage (about $1^{1}/_{2}$ pounds), finely shredded**
2 **large carrots, shredded**
$^{1}/_{2}$ **cup chopped red onion**
$^{1}/_{2}$ **cup mayonnaise**
$^{1}/_{3}$ **cup sour cream**
2 **tablespoons sugar**
2 **tablespoons chopped fresh cilantro**
$^{1}/_{4}$ **teaspoon hot sauce**
$^{1}/_{2}$ **cup toasted, chopped pecans**
Garnish: fresh cilantro sprigs

1. Combine shredded cabbage, carrot, and onion in a large bowl. Combine mayonnaise, sour cream, sugar, chopped cilantro, and hot sauce, stirring gently. Add to cabbage mixture; toss gently.
2. Cover and chill at least 1 hour. Sprinkle with pecans just before serving. Serve with a slotted spoon. Garnish, if desired. Yield: 6 servings.

Championship Cookies

Prep: 22 min. • **Cook:** 10 min. • **Other:** 30 min.

Serve up a batch of cookies loaded with chunky bits of candy as the grand-slam finish to Dad's special day.

$^{2}/_{3}$ **cup butter-flavored shortening**
$1^{1}/_{4}$ **cups firmly packed brown sugar**
1 **large egg**
$1^{1}/_{2}$ **cups all-purpose flour**
1 **teaspoon baking powder**
$^{1}/_{2}$ **teaspoon baking soda**
$^{1}/_{4}$ **teaspoon salt**
$^{1}/_{2}$ **teaspoon ground cinnamon**
$^{1}/_{2}$ **cup regular oats, uncooked**
4 **(2.07-ounce) chocolate-coated caramel-peanut nougat bars, coarsely chopped**
1 **teaspoon vanilla extract**

1. Beat shortening at medium speed with an electric mixer 2 minutes or until creamy; gradually add sugar, beating 5 minutes. Add egg, beating well.
2. Combine flour and next 5 ingredients. Add to shortening mixture, beating at low speed just until blended. Stir in chopped candy bars and vanilla. Chill dough 30 minutes.
3. Shape dough into $1^{1}/_{2}$-inch balls; place 2 inches apart on ungreased baking sheets. Bake at 350°F for 8 to 10 minutes (cookies will be soft). Cool slightly on baking sheets; remove to wire racks to cool completely. Yield: about 3 dozen.

Championship Cookies

burger bash

There's nothing like a good old-fashioned burger hot off the grill, and these are especially mouthwatering. The secret ingredient is vegetable juice. Top those burgers with spicy ketchup and grilled veggies, seasoned to perfection and cooked until slightly sweet and oh-so-tender.

Big Juicy Burgers

DIRECT • MEDIUM-HIGH
Prep: 12 min. • Cook: 22 min.

You can also shape these burgers into 12 patties for smaller, quarter-pound burgers.

2 (6-ounce) cans 100% vegetable juice
3 white sandwich bread slices, torn into pieces
3 pounds ground chuck or ground round
1 large egg
1 1/2 teaspoons salt
1 teaspoon pepper
10 hamburger buns
Vegetable cooking spray
Garnishes: sliced veggies, condiments

1. Microwave vegetable juice in a glass bowl at HIGH 1 minute; add sandwich bread pieces, and cool. Combine with hands.
2. Combine vegetable juice mixture, ground chuck, and next 3 ingredients. Shape into 10 patties, each, about 1 inch thick.
3. Grill patties over *Direct Medium-High* heat 8 to 10 minutes on each side or until the internal temperature reaches 160°F for medium.
4. Spray cut sides of buns with cooking spray; grill buns, cut sides down, 30 to 60 seconds or until lightly browned. Serve hamburgers on buns. Garnish, if desired. Yield: 10 servings.

Sweet-Hot Ketchup

Prep: 5 min. • Other: 1 hr.

Serve this ketchup with burgers, hot dogs, or any other cookout classic for more zing.

1 cup ketchup
1 teaspoon chipotle chile pepper seasoning
1 teaspoon grated lime zest
3 tablespoons fresh lime juice
2 tablespoons honey

1. Stir together all ingredients until blended. Cover and chill 1 hour. Yield: 1 1/3 cups.

Grilled Red Onions

DIRECT • MEDIUM
Prep: 10 min. • Cook: 10 min. • Other: 8 hrs.

4 medium red or sweet onions
1 1/2 cups dry white wine
2 to 4 tablespoons butter
1 teaspoon chopped fresh thyme
1/8 teaspoon pepper

1. Cut onions crosswise into 1/2-inch slices. Place slices in a shallow container; add wine. Cover and chill 8 hours, turning occasionally. Drain.
2. Melt butter in small saucepan; stir in thyme and pepper. Brush onion slices with butter mixture, reserving some for basting.
3. Grill onions over *Direct Medium* heat for 8 to 10 minutes, turning and basting often with reserved butter mixture. Yield: 8 servings.

Grilled Tomatoes

DIRECT • MEDIUM
Prep: 10 min. • Cook: 8 min.

Liven up your burgers by topping them with grilled tomato halves.

2 garlic cloves, minced
2 tablespoons olive oil
5 large tomatoes, cut in half crosswise
1/2 teaspoon salt
1/2 teaspoon pepper
1/2 cup chopped fresh basil

1. Stir together garlic and oil. Brush cut sides of tomato halves evenly with garlic mixture; sprinkle evenly with salt and pepper.
2. Grill tomato halves over *Direct Medium* heat 3 to 4 minutes on each side. Sprinkle evenly with basil. Yield: 10 servings.

Big Juicy Burgers

Grilled Red Onions

When the onions take on great grill marks, they're getting tender and ready to turn.

fourth of july beach party

Celebrate Independence Day at the beach with family and friends. Set up the mostly make-ahead meal right down by the water's edge so you can enjoy a beautiful sunset.

menu

Serves 8

Shrimp Cocktail

Catch-of-the-Day Hoagies

Red Onion Relish

Piña Colada Ice Cream

Shortbread Shells

Shrimp Cocktail

Prep: 15 min. • Cook: 5 min. • Other: 30 min.

2 quarts water
1 tablespoon salt
3 pounds unpeeled, large fresh shrimp
1 1/2 cups commercial cocktail sauce
1 1/2 tablespoons prepared horseradish
Lemon wedges (optional)

1. Bring water and salt to a boil; add shrimp, and cook 3 to 5 minutes. Drain; rinse with cold water. Chill. Peel shrimp, leaving tails on; devein shrimp, if desired. Cover and chill until ready to serve.
2. Combine cocktail sauce and horseradish, stirring well. Cover and chill until ready to serve. Serve shrimp with cocktail sauce and lemon wedges, if desired. Yield: 8 appetizer servings.

Catch-of-the-Day Hoagies

DIRECT • HIGH

Prep: 10 min. • Cook: 7 min. • Other: 30 min.

2 1/2 pounds grouper, amberjack, red snapper, or other firm-fleshed fish fillet
3/4 cup red wine vinegar
1/4 cup olive oil
1 tablespoon light brown sugar
2 tablespoons honey mustard
1/2 teaspoon freshly ground pepper
4 garlic cloves, minced
8 (6- to 7-inch) French bread loaves, split lengthwise
1/3 cup olive oil
Fresh Herb Mayonnaise
Red leaf lettuce
Red Onion Relish

1. Cut fish into 8 serving-size pieces, each about 1/2 inch thick, and place in a shallow dish. Combine vinegar and next 5 ingredients, stirring well. Pour mixture over fish. Cover and marinate in refrigerator 30 minutes.
2. Remove fish from marinade, discarding marinade. Grill fish over *Direct High* heat until opaque in the center, 4 to 6 minutes, turning once.
3. Brush cut sides of French bread loaves with olive oil. Grill bread, cut sides down, over *Direct High* heat until toasted, 30 to 60 seconds. Remove bread from grill, and wrap in aluminum foil. Keep warm until just before serving.

4. To serve, spread Fresh Herb Mayonnaise evenly on bottom of each French bread loaf. Place lettuce, grilled fish, and Red Onion Relish on bottom halves; replace tops. Yield: 8 servings.

Fresh Herb Mayonnaise

Prep: 5 min. • Other: 1 hr.

1 cup mayonnaise
1 tablespoon chopped fresh basil
1 tablespoon chopped fresh oregano
1 tablespoon chopped fresh thyme
1 large garlic clove, crushed

1. Combine all ingredients, stirring well. Cover and chill at least 1 hour. Yield: 1 cup.

Red Onion Relish

Prep: 5 min. • Cook: 29 min.

2 pounds red onions, thinly sliced
1/4 cup butter, melted
1/2 cup balsamic vinegar
3 tablespoons brown sugar
1/2 teaspoon freshly ground pepper

1. Cook onions in butter in a Dutch oven over medium heat 15 minutes or until very tender, stirring occasionally. Add vinegar, brown sugar, and pepper. Cook, uncovered, over medium heat 12 to 14 minutes or until liquid is absorbed, stirring occasionally. Remove from heat, and cool to room temperature. Yield: 1 1/2 cups.

Catch-of-the-Day
Hoagies with Red
Onion Relish

Paired with Shortbread Shells, this ice cream tastes even better than its namesake.

Piña Colada Ice Cream

Prep: 10 min. • Cook: 8 min. • Other: 2 hrs.

1 quart milk
1 1/2 cups sugar
1 cup cream of coconut
5 egg yolks, lightly beaten
1 quart half-and-half
1/2 cup flaked coconut
1/4 cup light rum
1 (15 1/4-ounce) can crushed pineapple in heavy syrup, drained

1. Combine first 3 ingredients in a large saucepan. Cook over medium heat, stirring constantly, until sugar dissolves. Gradually stir about one-fourth of hot milk mixture into yolks; add to remaining hot mixture, stirring constantly. Cook over medium heat, stirring constantly, 2 to 3 minutes or until thermometer reaches 160°F. Remove from heat; cool.
2. Stir in half-and-half, flaked coconut, and rum. Cover and chill custard thoroughly. Pour custard into freezer container of a 5-quart hand-turned or electric freezer. Freeze according to manufacturer's instructions. Remove dasher, and stir in crushed pineapple. Cover and pack freezer with additional ice and rock salt; let stand 1 hour before serving. Yield: about 1 gallon.

Shortbread Shells

Prep: 15 min. • Cook: 22 min.

These shells are the perfect size to hold a scoop of ice cream. Find scallop-shaped baking shells at kitchen supply stores.

2/3 cup butter, softened
3/4 cup sifted powdered sugar
1 1/2 teaspoons coconut extract
1 teaspoon vanilla extract
2 1/4 cups all-purpose flour
1/4 teaspoon salt
Vegetable cooking spray

1. Beat butter at medium speed with an electric mixer until creamy. Gradually add sugar, beating until light and fluffy. Add flavorings; beat well. Gradually stir in flour and salt.
2. Place 1 tablespoon of dough onto outside of each 2½-inch-wide scallop-shaped baking shell coated with cooking spray. Gently press dough over each shell, leaving ⅛-inch border around shell to allow for expansion during baking.
3. Place shells, dough side up, on ungreased baking sheets. Bake at 325°F for 20 to 22 minutes or until lightly browned. Cool completely on wire racks; carefully remove cookies from shells. Store cookies in an airtight container up to 1 week. Yield: 28 cookies.

short story

The secret of shortbread's buttery crumb lies in its simplicity. A basic blend of butter, sugar, and flour results in a taste far more than the sum of its parts. Good shortbread needs careful handling and precise baking.

Using scallop-shaped baking shells lets cookies mimic the beach party theme. You can also make simple shortbread bars by pressing dough into an ungreased jellyroll pan. Prick dough at 1-inch intervals with a fork and score into bars. Cover and chill at least 2 hours. Bake at 325°F for 35 minutes. Cool in pan on a wire rack 5 minutes; cut into bars. Cool completely before removing from pan.

Shortbread Shells carry out the beach party theme as dippers for Piña Colada Ice Cream. Tiny straw hats with red, white, and blue ribbons suspended from wooden picks make a playful garnish.

Piña Colada
Ice Cream and
Shortbread Shells

salads for supper

Whether you're into the low-carb craze or just like the smoky flavor the grill imparts to these salads, you can have a refreshing dinner on the double with these recipes.

Grilled Steak Salad Niçoise

Prep: 20 min. • Cook: 16 min.

4 medium new potatoes, cut into $^1/_4$-inch slices

Reserved vinaigrette from Flank Steak with Dijon Vinaigrette (recipe on facing page)

$^1/_4$ pound small green beans, trimmed

6 cups gourmet salad greens

1 $^1/_2$ pounds grilled Flank Steak with Dijon Vinaigrette, thinly sliced (recipe on facing page)

4 plum tomatoes, each cut into 6 wedges

16 kalamata olives

2 hard-cooked eggs, quartered

1. Cook potatoes in boiling water to cover in a large saucepan 10 to 12 minutes or until tender; drain and toss with ½ cup of reserved vinaigrette. Set aside.

2. Cook green beans in boiling water to cover 3 to 4 minutes or until crisp-tender; drain. Plunge beans into ice water to stop the cooking process; drain. Pat dry with paper towels, and set aside.

3. Toss salad greens with ¼ cup of remaining vinaigrette, and place on 4 serving plates. Arrange steak, green beans, potato, tomato, olives, and egg on salad greens. Drizzle with remaining vinaigrette, and serve immediately. Yield: 4 servings.

flank steak flavors

Flank steak's ample surface area makes it a perfect meat for picking up complex flavors. Marinades, rubs, and sauces are all easy ways to take advantage of this quality. Because it's relatively inexpensive, feel free to experiment with new flavors. This tasty, versatile cut is a great addition to last-minute meals, make-ahead entrées, sandwiches, and salads.

Grilled Steak Salad Niçoise

3. Remove steak from marinade, discarding marinade. Allow steak to stand at room temperature for 20 to 30 minutes before grilling.
4. Grill steak over *Direct High* heat 8 to 10 minutes, turning once. Remove from the grill and let rest for 5 minutes. Cut diagonally across grain into ¼-inch-thick slices. Yield: 6 servings.

Fiery Thai Beef Salad

DIRECT • HIGH
Prep: 25 min. • Cook: 10 min. • Other: 5 min.

1 pound flank steak
¹/₄ teaspoon salt
¹/₈ teaspoon black pepper
Extra-virgin olive oil
¹/₃ cup fresh lime juice
¹/₄ cup chopped fresh cilantro
2 tablespoons light brown
  sugar
1 tablespoon water
1 tablespoon Thai fish sauce
5 garlic cloves, minced
2 Thai, hot red, or serrano chiles,
  seeded and minced
6 cups torn romaine lettuce
1³/₄ cups quartered cherry
  tomatoes
1 cup thinly sliced red onion,
  separated into rings
¹/₄ cup coarsely chopped fresh mint
2 tablespoons thinly sliced, peeled
  fresh lemon grass

1. Allow the steak to stand at room temperature for 20 to 30 minutes before grilling. Sprinkle both sides of steak with salt and pepper. Lightly spray or brush both sides of the steak with olive oil.
2. Meanwhile, combine lime juice and next 6 ingredients for dressing in a bowl; stir well with a whisk, and set aside.
3. Grill the steak over Direct High heat for 8 to 10 minutes, turning once. Remove from the grill and let rest for 5 minutes. Cut steak diagonally across grain into thin slices; cut into 2-inch pieces.
4. Combine steak, lettuce, and next 4 ingredients in a large bowl; add dressing, tossing to coat. Yield: 4 servings.

Steak and Blue Cheese Quesadilla Salad

Steak and Blue Cheese Quesadilla Salad

Prep: 15 min. • Cook: 8 min.

These quesadillas are generously stuffed. To make cutting easier, let them stand a minute or so after cooking, then cut with kitchen shears.

¹/₂ cup crumbled blue cheese
4 (8-inch) flour tortillas
¹/₂ pound grilled Flank Steak
  with Dijon Vinaigrette, thinly
  sliced (recipe at right)
Vegetable cooking spray
¹/₂ cup bottled vinaigrette
10 cups torn red leaf lettuce
1 cup vertically sliced red onion
2 large tomatoes, each cut into
  8 wedges

1. Sprinkle ¼ cup cheese evenly over each of 2 tortillas. Divide steak evenly over cheese; top with the remaining tortillas.
2. Heat a large nonstick skillet coated with cooking spray over medium heat. Cook quesadillas 4 minutes on each side or until golden brown. Remove quesadillas from pan, and cut each into 8 wedges. Combine the vinaigrette, lettuce, onion, and tomato in a large bowl; toss well. Divide salad evenly among 4 plates; accompany each serving with 4 quesadilla wedges. Yield: 4 servings.

Flank Steak with Dijon Vinaigrette

DIRECT • HIGH
Prep: 10 min. • Cook: 10 min. • Other: 1¹/₂ hrs.

Serve this flank steak as the cornerstone of a meat-and-potatoes dinner or the make-ahead meat for the Niçoise salad and the quesadilla salad that precede. One recipe of the flank makes enough for both salads.

2 pounds flank steak
1 (16-ounce) bottle vinaigrette
2 tablespoons Dijon mustard
2 teaspoons anchovy paste
  (optional)

1. Score steak diagonally across grain at ¾-inch intervals.
2. Whisk together vinaigrette, mustard, and, if desired, anchovy paste. Pour ½ cup mixture in a shallow dish or zip-top freezer bag; reserve remaining mixture for Grilled Steak Salad Niçoise or other uses. Add flank steak to dish or bag, cover or seal, and chill 1 hour, turning occasionally.

Grilled Salmon over
Gourmet Greens

Grilled Salmon over Gourmet Greens

DIRECT • HIGH

Prep: 15 min. • Cook: 11 min.

1 cucumber, peeled, seeded, and
  diced
1/4 cup plain low-fat yogurt
1 1/4 teaspoons grated lime zest
2 tablespoons fresh lime juice
1 1/2 teaspoons chopped fresh
  parsley
1 1/2 teaspoons chopped fresh
  chives
1/4 teaspoon black pepper
1 garlic clove, halved
4 (6-ounce) salmon fillets (about
  1 inch thick)
1 teaspoon black pepper
1/2 teaspoon salt
Extra-virgin olive oil
4 cups gourmet salad greens
  (about 4 ounces)
1 cup loosely packed fresh basil
  leaves, torn in pieces
1/2 cup cubed peeled ripe mango

1. Combine first 8 ingredients in a blender or food processor; process until almost smooth. Set dressing aside.

2. Sprinkle the salmon with 1 teaspoon pepper and salt, and generously brush or spray both sides with olive oil. Grill the fillets, flesh side down, over *Direct High* heat until you can lift the fillets with tongs without them sticking to the grate, 7 to 8 minutes. Turn, skin side down, and finish cooking for 2 to 3 minutes more. Slide a spatula between the skin and flesh and transfer the fillets to a plate. Break fish into chunks.

3. Place greens and basil in a large bowl; add 1/4 cup cucumber dressing, tossing well.

4. Arrange salad on 4 plates. Divide salmon chunks evenly among salads; top each serving evenly with cucumber dressing and mango. Yield: 4 servings.

Fruited Tuna-Salad Pita Sandwiches

DIRECT • HIGH

Prep: 15 min. • Cook: 10 min.

1 teaspoon fresh lemon juice
Dash of black pepper
1/2 teaspoon salt
1 (8-ounce) tuna steak (1 inch thick)
Extra-virgin olive oil
1 hard-cooked egg, diced
1/4 cup diced celery
1/4 cup raisins
2 tablespoons minced green
  onions
3 tablespoons mayonnaise
1 teaspoon Dijon mustard
1 (8-ounce) can unsweetened
  pineapple tidbits, drained
2 (5-inch) whole wheat pitas, cut
  in half
1 1/3 cups torn Bibb lettuce
8 (1/4-inch-thick) tomato slices

1. Sprinkle lemon juice, pepper, and salt over tuna. Lightly brush or spray both sides of tuna steak with olive oil. Grill over *Direct High* heat until opaque throughout and firm to the touch, 8 to 10 minutes, turning once. Coarsely chop tuna.

2. Combine tuna, egg, celery, and next 5 ingredients in a bowl. Line each pita half with ⅓ cup lettuce and 2 tomato slices. Divide tuna mixture evenly among pita halves. Yield: 4 servings.

Grilled Pork Cosmopolitan Salad

DIRECT • MEDIUM
Prep: 30 min. • Cook: 20 min. • Other: 30 min.

This tasty recipe plays off the flavors of the fashionable, colorful Cosmopolitan cocktail.

¼ cup jellied cranberry sauce
¼ cup orange marmalade
⅓ cup orange juice
¼ cup fresh lime juice
¼ cup peanut oil
2¼ teaspoons salt, divided
2 tablespoons vodka
1 tablespoon minced or grated
    fresh ginger
2 (1-pound) pork tenderloins
2 teaspoons lemon-pepper
    seasoning
½ teaspoon ground cayenne
    pepper
2 (10-ounce) packages European
    blend salad greens
½ cup dried cranberries
1 (8-ounce) can mandarin
    oranges, drained

1. Whisk together cranberry sauce and marmalade in a small saucepan over low heat until melted. Remove from heat. Whisk in orange juice, lime juice, and oil. Reserve ½ cup of cranberry mixture; add ¼ teaspoon salt to reserved mixture, and set aside.
2. Pour remaining cranberry mixture into a shallow dish or zip-top freezer bag; add vodka, ginger, and pork, turning to coat all sides. Cover or seal, and marinate at room temperature for 20 to 30 minutes before grilling. Remove

pork from marinade; discard marinade in the dish or bag.
3. Stir together remaining 2 teaspoons salt, lemon-pepper seasoning, and ground cayenne pepper; sprinkle evenly over pork.
4. Grill over *Direct Medium* heat until the centers are barely pink and the internal temperature reaches 155°F, 15 to 20 minutes, turning once. Remove from the grill, loosely cover with foil, and let rest for 5 minutes. Cut pork diagonally into ¼-inch-thick slices.
5. Toss together salad greens, cranberries, and oranges with reserved ½ cup cranberry mixture; top with pork. Yield: 6 to 8 servings.

Buffalo Chicken Salad with Blue Cheese-Buttermilk Dressing

DIRECT • MEDIUM
Prep: 15 min. • Cook: 27 min. • Other: 1 hr.

The flavors of Buffalo wings and blue cheese dip team up in this salad.

1 tablespoon paprika
1½ tablespoons olive oil
2 tablespoons hot sauce
6 (4-ounce) skinned and boned
    chicken breasts
1 large carrot
1 celery rib
3 cups cubed red potato
6 cups shredded romaine lettuce
2 cups cherry tomato halves
Blue Cheese-Buttermilk Dressing

1. Combine first 3 ingredients in a large dish. Add chicken, tossing to coat. Cover and marinate in refrigerator 30 minutes to 1 hour.
2. Cut carrot and celery lengthwise into 12 thin strips using a vegetable peeler. Place strips in a bowl of ice water. Let stand 30 minutes.
3. Place potato in a saucepan; cover with water. Bring to a boil; cook 15 minutes or until tender. Drain; cool.
4. Remove chicken from marinade; discard marinade. Grill the chicken over *Direct Medium* heat until the juices run clear and

the meat is no longer pink in the center, 8 to 12 minutes, turning once. Cut chicken diagonally across grain into thin slices. Set aside.
5. Arrange lettuce on a large platter. Top with potato, carrot and celery strips, chicken, and tomato halves. Serve with Blue Cheese-Buttermilk Dressing. Yield: 6 servings.

Blue Cheese-Buttermilk Dressing

Prep: 10 min.

½ cup buttermilk
½ cup plain low-fat yogurt
3 tablespoons white wine vinegar
1 teaspoon sugar
½ teaspoon salt
½ teaspoon coarsely ground
    pepper
½ cup thinly sliced green onions
½ cup crumbled blue cheese

1. Whisk together first 6 ingredients in a bowl until blended. Stir in green onions and cheese. Yield: 1½ cups.

There's no better time than summer to savor these garden-fresh salads made into meals by adding freshly grilled meats or fish.

the skinny on grilling

Grilling, a naturally healthy way to cook, is a perfect match for the health-conscious chef. Rely on these flavorful recipes to keep you full and fit—no one has to know they're good for you!

Tilapia in Corn Husks

DIRECT • MEDIUM

Prep: 25 min. • Cook: 30 min.

6 large ears fresh corn with husks
$^1/_2$ cup water
$^1/_4$ cup chopped onion
1 (4$^1/_2$-ounce) can chopped green chiles, drained
1 (2-ounce) jar diced pimiento, drained
1 tablespoon fresh lime juice
$^1/_4$ teaspoon salt
$^1/_4$ teaspoon ground cumin
$^1/_4$ teaspoon black pepper
6 (4-ounce) tilapia fillets
Vegetable cooking spray
Lime wedges (optional)

1. Peel back husks from corn, leaving husks attached to stem. Remove corn cobs; remove and discard the corn silk. Cut 6 (8-inch) pieces of string. Place husks and string in a large bowl; add water to cover. Set aside.

2. Cut enough corn from cobs to measure ¾ cup, and reserve remaining corn for another use. Bring corn and ½ cup water to a boil over medium-high heat in a saucepan. Cover, reduce heat, and simmer 10 minutes or until tender; drain. Stir in onion and next 6 ingredients; set aside.

3. Drain husks and string; pat dry with paper towels. Place fillets inside husks near stems; top evenly with corn mixture. Pull husks back over fillets; tie tips with string.

4. Lightly spray husk packets on all sides with cooking spray. Grill husk packets over *Direct Medium* heat until fish is opaque in the center, 15 to 20 minutes, turning once. Remove strings from packets before serving. Serve fish with lime wedges, if desired. Yield: 6 servings.

Note: To bake fish without corn husks, place fillets in a 13- x 9-inch pan. Top with corn mixture. Bake at 350°F for 15 minutes or until fish flakes with a fork.

Per Serving: Cal: 140; Fat: 3.1g; Pro: 22g; Carb: 6.3g; Fib: 1g; Chol: 80m; Iron: 1.4mg; Sod: 235mg; Calc: 74mg

Tilapia in Corn Husks

Grilled Grouper with Avocado Aïoli

DIRECT • HIGH
Prep: 15 min. • Cook: 10 min. • Other: 30 min.

1 teaspoon grated lemon zest
1/4 cup fresh lemon juice
1/4 cup lite soy sauce
2 tablespoons water
1/4 teaspoon chicken bouillon
    granules
2 garlic cloves, pressed
8 (4-ounce) grouper fillets
    (3/4 inch thick)
Extra-virgin olive oil
Avocado Aïoli
24 (1/4-inch-thick) avocado slices
8 (1/8-inch-thick) lemon slices,
    quartered
Garnish: fresh cilantro sprigs

1. Combine first 6 ingredients in a shallow dish or large zip-top freezer bag; add fish. Cover or seal, and chill 30 minutes, turning once.
2. Remove the fillets from the bag and reserve the marinade. Pour the marinade into a small saucepan, bring to a boil, and boil for 1 full minute.
3. Lightly brush or spray both sides of fillets with oil. Grill over *Direct High* heat until opaque in the center, 8 to 10 minutes, turning once and basting often with boiled marinade. Serve with Avocado Aïoli, avocado slices, and lemon quarters. Garnish, if desired. Yield: 8 servings.

Avocado Aïoli

Prep: 7 min.

1/4 cup mashed ripe avocado
1 tablespoon minced fresh
    cilantro
1 garlic clove, pressed
3 tablespoons nonfat
    mayonnaise
2 tablespoons lime juice

1. Process all ingredients in a blender until smooth, stopping to scrape down sides. Yield: 1/2 cup.

Per Serving: Cal: 181.3g; Fat 7.7g; Pro: 23.3g; Carb 4.7g; Fib 1.8g; Chol 42mg; Iron 1.4mg; Sod 487mg; Calc 38.3mg

Lime Chicken with Grilled Pineapple

DIRECT • MEDIUM
Prep: 15 min. • Cook: 13 min. • Other: 2 hrs.

Lime juice adds lots of zing, so you don't need to add oil or butter to get raves for your cooking.

6 (4-ounce) skinned and boned
    chicken breasts
1 teaspoon salt, divided
1 teaspoon black pepper, divided
1 cup fresh lime juice, divided
2 jalapeño peppers, seeded,
    minced, and divided
1/2 cup pineapple juice
2 garlic cloves, minced
1/2 cup tequila (optional)
1 pineapple, peeled, cored, and
    cut horizontally in half
1 orange, sliced 1/4 inch thick
2 tablespoons honey
1/2 teaspoon grated lime zest

1. Place chicken between 2 sheets of heavy-duty plastic wrap, and flatten to a 1/4-inch thickness, using a meat mallet or rolling pin. Sprinkle evenly with 1/2 teaspoon salt and 1/2 teaspoon pepper.
2. Whisk together remaining 1/2 teaspoon salt, remaining 1/2 teaspoon pepper, 3/4 cup lime juice, 1 minced jalapeño pepper, pineapple juice, garlic, and, if desired, tequila in a shallow bowl. Add chicken. Cover; chill 2 hours. Drain chicken, discarding the marinade.
3. Grill the chicken over *Direct Medium* heat until the juices run clear and the meat is no longer pink in the center, 3 to 5 minutes, turning once.
4. Grill pineapple and orange slices over *Direct Medium* heat until browned in spots and warm throughout, 6 to 8 minutes, turning once. Coarsely chop pineapple, and place in a medium bowl. Stir in remaining 1/4 cup lime juice, remaining 1 minced jalapeño, honey, and lime zest. Serve with chicken and grilled orange slices. Yield: 6 servings.

Per Serving: Cal: 209; Fat: 1.6g; Pro: 27g; Carb: 20.1g; Fib: 1.8g; Chol: 66mg; Iron: 1.2mg; Sod 366mg; Calc: 37mg

Tequila and fresh lime juice play out a margarita theme in this zesty marinade.

Grilled Venison Steaks

DIRECT • HIGH
Prep: 5 min. • Cook: 10 min. • Other: 4 hrs.

Serve these steaks with mashed potatoes and asparagus for a heart-smart meal.

4 (4-ounce) lean, boneless
    venison loin steaks (1 inch thick)
1 cup cranberry-orange crushed
    fruit, divided
1/2 cup dry red wine
2 tablespoons Dijon mustard
2 teaspoons minced garlic (about
    4 cloves)
2 teaspoons dried rosemary,
    crushed
1/2 teaspoon black pepper
Vegetable cooking spray

1. Trim fat from steaks. Place steaks in a large zip-top freezer bag. Combine 1/2 cup cranberry-orange crushed fruit, wine, and next 4 ingredients; pour over steaks. Seal bag; turn to coat steaks. Marinate in refrigerator 4 to 8 hours, turning bag occasionally. Remove steaks from marinade, discarding marinade in the bag.
2. Lightly spray both sides of the steaks with cooking spray. Grill the steaks over *Direct High* heat until the internal temperature reaches 145°F for medium-rare, 8 to 10 minutes, turning once. Remove from the grill and let rest for 3 to 5 minutes. Serve warm with remaining 1/2 cup cranberry-orange crushed fruit. Yield: 4 servings.

Per Serving: Cal: 236; Fat: 2.1g; Pro: 26.7g; Carb: 25.3g; Fib: 0.2g; Chol: 67mg; Iron: 3.8mg; Sod: 156mg; Calc: 18mg

no-fuss, no-muss kabob dinners

Kabobs let you relish the joys of summer grilling—a cool kitchen; super-quick, super-good suppers; and easy cleanup.

Rosemary-Skewered Swordfish

DIRECT • HIGH
Prep: 20 min. • Cook: 10 min. • Other: 35 min.

Use prebaked potatoes so they can cook as fast as the fish.

8 (8- to 10-inch) rosemary
  branches
2 garlic cloves, minced
$^1/_2$ teaspoon black pepper
$^1/_4$ teaspoon salt
1 teaspoon grated lemon zest
1 tablespoon fresh lemon juice
$^1/_3$ cup olive oil
$1^1/_2$ pounds swordfish, cut into
  1-inch pieces
2 baking potatoes, baked, chilled,
  and cut into 1-inch pieces
1 pint cherry tomatoes
1 red onion, cut into wedges

1. Strip rosemary leaves from branches, leaving 2 inches of leaves at tip of stems; chop leaves to measure 2 tablespoons. Soak stems in water 20 minutes.
2. Whisk together chopped rosemary, garlic, and next 5 ingredients in a small bowl. Set aside.
3. Alternately thread fish, potatoes, tomatoes, and onion onto rosemary skewers. Place in a 13- x 9-inch baking dish, and add marinade. Turn skewers gently in marinade to coat. Let stand 15 minutes.
4. Grill over *Direct High* heat until the fish is opaque throughout, 8 to 10 minutes, turning once. Yield: 4 servings.

Asian Kabob Smorgasbord

DIRECT • MEDIUM and HIGH
Prep: 10 min. • Cook: 16 min. • Other: 8 hrs.

Please all your family with their choice of beef, chicken, seafood, or veggie kabobs that bathe in an Asian marinade before hitting the grill.

1 cup olive oil
$^1/_2$ cup low-sodium soy sauce
1 tablespoon light brown sugar
1 tablespoon sesame seeds,
  toasted
1 tablespoon minced fresh ginger
1 tablespoon Worcestershire
  sauce
2 tablespoons fresh lime juice
1 teaspoon dark sesame oil
$^1/_2$ teaspoon dried crushed red
  pepper
$^1/_4$ teaspoon freshly ground
  black pepper
4 garlic cloves, minced
Choice of beef, chicken, seafood,
  or vegetable kabobs (see below)

1. Whisk together first 11 ingredients in a large bowl. Use to marinate beef, chicken, seafood, and vegetable kabobs. Each variation that follows uses one batch of the marinade; increase the marinade accordingly for each kabob variation you choose. Yield: $1^3/_4$ cups marinade and 4 to 6 servings.

For beef kabobs, cut 2 pounds sirloin steak into 2-inch cubes. Cut 2 large bell peppers into 2-inch pieces. Rinse and pat dry 1 (8-ounce) package whole, small button mushrooms. Pour $1^1/_2$ cups marinade into a large zip-top freezer bag. Add steak cubes, pepper pieces, and mushrooms to bag; marinate in refrigerator 8 hours or overnight.

Remove ingredients from marinade, discarding marinade in the bag. Alternate steak cubes, pepper pieces, and whole mushrooms on 12-inch skewers. Grill the kabobs over *Direct High* heat until the meat is medium-rare, 8 to 10 minutes, turning four times and basting with additional $^1/_4$ cup marinade. Yield: 4 to 6 servings.

For chicken kabobs, cut 2 pounds skinned and boned chicken breasts into 2-inch pieces. Cut 2 large bell peppers into 2-inch pieces. Pour $1^1/_2$ cups marinade into a large zip-top freezer bag. Add chicken pieces and pepper pieces to bag; marinate in refrigerator 8 hours or overnight.

Remove ingredients from marinade, discarding marinade in the bag. Cut 1 fresh pineapple into 2-inch chunks. Alternate chicken pieces, pepper pieces, and pineapple chunks on 12-inch skewers. Grill the kabobs over *Direct Medium* heat until the meat is firm and the juices run clear, 8 to 10 minutes, turning once and basting with additional $^1/_4$ cup marinade. Yield: 4 to 6 servings.

For seafood kabobs, place 1 pound snow peas in a wire-mesh basket with handle and dip in boiling water 30 seconds. Immediately hold basket under cold running water to stop the cooking process; set aside. Peel and devein 1 pound shrimp. Pour 1½ cups marinade into a large zip-top freezer bag. Add snow peas, shrimp, and 1 pound small fresh sea scallops to bag; marinate in refrigerator 2 to 4 hours.

Remove ingredients from marinade, discarding marinade in the bag. Wrap 1 snow pea around each scallop. Cut 1 fresh pineapple into 1-inch chunks. Alternate scallops, shrimp, and pineapple chunks on 12-inch skewers (note: thread the scallops through their sides so they lie flat on the grill and thread each shrimp through both its head and tail so it doesn't spin around). Grill the kabobs over *Direct High* heat until the shrimp and scallops are just opaque in the center and firm to the touch, about 4 minutes, turning once and basting with additional ¼ cup marinade. Yield: 4 to 6 servings.

For vegetable kabobs, cut 3 large bell peppers into 2-inch pieces. Slice 2 large zucchini crosswise into ½-inch slices. Rinse and pat dry 1 (8-ounce) package whole, small button mushrooms. Pour 1½ cups marinade into a large zip-top freezer bag. Add pepper pieces, zucchini, and mushrooms to bag; marinate in refrigerator 8 hours or overnight.

Remove ingredients from marinade, discarding marinade in the bag. Alternate pepper pieces, zucchini slices, and whole mushrooms on 12-inch skewers. Grill the kabobs over *Direct Medium* heat until tender but not limp, about 8 minutes, turning once and basting with additional ¼ cup marinade. Yield: 4 to 6 servings.

> Enjoy the tastes of Morocco with every bite of these savory lamb kabobs.

Lamb Veggie Kabobs

Lamb-Veggie Kabobs

DIRECT • HIGH

Prep: 20 min. • Cook: 11 min. • Other: 8 hrs.

2 pounds lean, boneless leg of lamb
¼ cup red wine vinegar
¼ cup fresh lemon juice
¼ cup extra-virgin olive oil
2 tablespoons minced fresh parsley
½ teaspoon salt
½ teaspoon black pepper
½ teaspoon ground cumin
3 garlic cloves, minced
1 (1-pound) eggplant, unpeeled
1 medium zucchini
1 large sweet onion
1 medium red bell pepper
1 medium yellow bell pepper
8 large fresh mushrooms
Extra-virgin olive oil

1. Cut lamb into 1½-inch cubes. Combine vinegar and next 7 ingredients in a shallow dish or zip-top freezer bag; add lamb. Cover or seal, and refrigerate, turning occasionally, 8 hours.

2. Cut eggplant lengthwise into quarters; cut each quarter crosswise into 4 pieces. Cut zucchini lengthwise in half; cut each half crosswise into 4 pieces. Cut onion into 8 wedges. Cut each bell pepper into 8 pieces, and set aside.

3. Alternate 2 eggplant pieces, 1 zucchini piece, and 1 onion wedge on 8 (10-inch) skewers; set aside.

4. Remove lamb from marinade and reserve the marinade. Pour the marinade into a small saucepan, bring to a boil, and boil for 1 full minute. Alternate 3 lamb cubes, 1 red bell pepper piece, 1 yellow bell pepper piece, and 1 mushroom on 8 (10-inch) skewers.

5. Lightly brush or spray kabobs with oil. Grill eggplant kabobs over *Direct High* heat 8 to 10 minutes, basting with boiled marinade and turning once. At same time, grill lamb kabobs until the meat is medium-rare, 8 to 10 minutes, turning and basting with boiled marinade. Yield: 8 servings.

just wing it!

Tangy chicken wings give parties flair. For wings that look as good as they taste, sear them first for appealing grill marks. When the marinade is high in sugar or fat, finish cooking the wings over indirect heat to prevent flare-ups.

Buffalo Hot Wings

DIRECT • MEDIUM
Prep: 8 min. • Cook: 15 min.

16 chicken wings (about 4 pounds)
Salt
Black pepper
Extra-virgin olive oil
1/2 cup butter, melted
1/2 cup hot sauce
Ranch dressing

1. Cut off wing tips, and discard; cut wings in half at joint. Sprinkle wings with salt and pepper to taste; lightly brush or spray wings with oil.
2. Grill wings over *Direct Medium* heat until meat is no longer pink at the bone, about 15 minutes, turning occasionally.
3. Whisk together butter and hot sauce. Add cooked wings to sauce, tossing to coat. Serve with dressing. Yield: 4 to 6 servings.

Balsamic Chicken Wings

SEAR: MEDIUM
GRILL: INDIRECT • MEDIUM
Prep: 8 min. • Cook: 18 min. • Other: 2 hrs.

10 chicken wings (about 2 1/2 pounds)
1/2 cup balsamic vinegar
1/4 cup extra-virgin olive oil
3/4 teaspoon Greek seasoning
3 green onions, thinly sliced
Extra-virgin olive oil
Creamy feta dressing
Cucumber sticks

1. Cut off wing tips, and discard; cut wings in half at joint. Combine chicken and next 4 ingredients in a large zip-top freezer bag. Seal bag; shake gently. Marinate in refrigerator 2 hours, turning occasionally.

2. Remove chicken from marinade; discard marinade. Lightly brush or spray wings with oil. Sear over *Direct Medium* heat until well marked, 6 to 8 minutes, turning once. Continue grilling over *Indirect Medium* heat until the meat is no longer pink at the bone, 8 to 10 minutes. Serve warm with dressing and cucumber sticks. Yield: 2 to 3 servings.

Grilled Honey Chicken Wings

SEAR: MEDIUM
GRILL: INDIRECT • MEDIUM
Prep: 8 min. • Cook: 18 min. • Other: 2 hrs.

12 chicken wings (about 3 pounds)
1/2 cup soy sauce
1/4 cup dry sherry
1/4 cup honey
1/4 teaspoon garlic powder
1/4 teaspoon ground ginger
3 tablespoons butter
Extra-virgin olive oil
Blue cheese dressing

1. Cut off wing tips, and discard; cut wings in half at joint. Combine soy sauce and next 5 ingredients in a saucepan; cook, stirring constantly, over medium heat just until thoroughly heated. Reserve 1/4 cup marinade for basting. Allow remaining marinade to cool to room temperature. Pour into a large zip-top freezer bag; add chicken, and seal. Refrigerate 2 hours, turning occasionally.
2. Remove chicken from marinade; discard marinade. Lightly brush or spray the wings with oil. Sear over *Direct Medium* heat until

well marked, 6 to 8 minutes, turning once. Baste with reserved marinade; continue grilling over *Indirect Medium* heat until the meat is no longer pink at the bone, 8 to 10 minutes, basting often with the reserved marinade. Serve warm with blue cheese dressing. Yield: 3 to 4 servings.

Curried Chicken Wings

SEAR: MEDIUM
GRILL: INDIRECT • MEDIUM
Prep: 8 min. • Cook: 18 min. • Other: 2 hrs.

10 chicken wings (about 2 1/2 pounds)
1/4 cup butter, melted
1/4 cup honey
3 tablespoons prepared mustard
1 teaspoon salt
1 to 1 1/2 teaspoons curry powder
1/8 teaspoon ground cayenne pepper
Extra-virgin olive oil
Bottled chutney

1. Cut off wing tips, and discard; cut wings in half at joint. Combine butter and next 5 ingredients in a large zip-top freezer bag; add chicken, and seal. Refrigerate 2 hours, turning chicken occasionally.
2. Remove chicken from marinade; discard marinade. Lightly brush or spray wings with oil. Sear over *Direct Medium* heat until well marked, 6 to 8 minutes, turning once. Continue grilling over *Indirect Medium* heat until the meat is no longer pink at the bone, 8 to 10 minutes. Serve warm with chutney, if desired. Yield: 2 to 3 servings.

Asian Chicken Wings

Asian Chicken Wings

SEAR: MEDIUM

GRILL: INDIRECT • MEDIUM

Prep: 8 min. • Cook: 18 min. • Other: 4 hrs.

10 chicken wings (about 2¹/₂ pounds)

¹/₂ cup red plum sauce

¹/₄ cup soy sauce

1 to 1¹/₂ teaspoons Chinese mustard

1 tablespoon dark sesame oil

1 teaspoon dried crushed red pepper

Extra-virgin olive oil

Toasted sesame seeds

Sugar snap peas

Chinese mustard

Red plum sauce

1. Cut off wing tips, and discard; cut wings in half at joint. Combine plum sauce and next 4 ingredients in a large zip-top freezer bag; add chicken, and seal. Refrigerate 3 to 4 hours, turning chicken occasionally.

2. Remove chicken from marinade; discard marinade. Lightly brush or spray wings with oil. Sear over *Direct Medium* heat until well marked, 6 to 8 minutes, turning once. Continue grilling over *Indirect Medium* heat until the meat is no longer pink at the bone, 8 to 10 minutes. Sprinkle with sesame seeds; serve with sugar snap peas and additional Chinese mustard or additional plum sauce. Yield: 2 to 3 servings.

Tandoori Chicken Wings

SEAR: MEDIUM

GRILL: INDIRECT • MEDIUM

Prep: 11 min. • Cook: 18 min. • Other: 2 hrs.

10 chicken wings (about 2¹/₂ pounds)

1 (8-ounce) container plain low-fat yogurt

1¹/₂ tablespoons tandoori spice

¹/₂ teaspoon salt

2 tablespoons fresh lemon juice

¹/₂ medium onion, sliced

1. Cut off wing tips, and discard; cut wings in half at joint. Make small slits in chicken with a sharp knife. Combine yogurt, tandoori spice, and salt in a large zip-top freezer bag; add chicken, and seal. Refrigerate at least 2 hours, turning chicken occasionally.

2. Remove chicken from marinade; discard marinade. Sear over *Direct Medium* heat until well marked, 6 to 8 minutes, turning once. Continue grilling over *Indirect Medium* heat until the meat is no longer pink at the bone, 8 to 10 minutes. Transfer chicken wings to a serving platter. Sprinkle lemon juice over onion slices; toss gently to coat. Arrange over chicken. Yield: 2 to 3 servings.

mix-and-match cookbook

On the grill or in
the oven, these recipes
are sure to please.

for starters

While everyone lingers around the grill they'll need munchies to nibble on. You can make any of these appetizers ahead so you can enjoy the party, too.

Smoky Pecans

INDIRECT • MEDIUM
Prep: 10 min. • Cook: 1 hr. • Other: 30 min.

2 pounds pecan halves
1/2 cup unsalted butter, melted
1 teaspoon salt
Hickory wood chips, soaked in
    water for at least 30 minutes

1. Stir together pecans, butter, and salt in a 24- x 12-inch pan.
2. Follow the grill's instructions for using wood chips. Place pan on cooking grate. Grill pecans over *Indirect Medium* heat until golden, about 1 hour, stirring once or twice. Yield: 2 pounds.

Note: Use a baking pan that fits your grill if the 24- x 12-inch pan is too large.

smoke cooking is easy

Long, slow cooking gives you time to relax outdoors and smoke from wood chips wraps food in a blanket, sealing in the natural juices. If you don't have a smoker, your grill with a lid and a pan of water placed under the food works well. The simmering water keeps foods moist and the flavored wood chips (found near the charcoal in most grocery stores) make grill flavors and aromas something you won't soon forget.

Smoky Pecans

Easy Smoked Cheddar

Easy Smoked Cheddar

INDIRECT • LOW
Prep: 10 min. • Cook: 1 hr. • Other: 30 min.

Two blocks of cheese stacked on top of each other meld into one large chunk of cheese over the smoldering wood chips. Wrapping the blocks in cheesecloth fashions a rustic look.

2 (16-ounce) blocks Cheddar
    cheese
Vegetable cooking spray
Hickory wood chips, soaked in
    water for at least 30 minutes

1. Place 1 cheese block on top of the other; coat with cooking spray. Place lengthwise in center of a 24-inch piece of cheesecloth. Tightly wrap cheesecloth around stacked cheese. Place wrapped cheese crosswise in center of another 24-inch piece of cheesecloth; wrap tightly.
2. Follow the grill's instructions for using wood chips. Place wrapped cheese, seam side down, on cooking grate. Grill over *Indirect Low* heat for 1 hour. Remove from the grill and let rest for 10 minutes. Serve warm or cover and chill. If chilled, let come to room temperature before serving. Yield: 2 pounds (about 16 servings).

Artichoke
Cheesecake

Artichoke Cheesecake

Prep: 25 min. • Cook: 50 min. • Other: 2 hrs.

$^1/_4$ cup fine, dry breadcrumbs
$^1/_4$ cup grated Parmesan cheese
2 tablespoons dried Italian
    seasoning
2 (8-ounce) packages cream
    cheese, softened
1 cup crumbled feta cheese
3 large eggs
1 (8-ounce) container sour cream
1 (14-ounce) can artichoke
    hearts, drained
$^3/_4$ cup chopped red bell pepper
$^3/_4$ cup chopped green bell
    pepper
$^3/_4$ cup chopped green onions
    (including $^1/_2$-inch green tops)
1 large garlic clove, pressed
1 teaspoon dried tarragon
1 teaspoon dried basil

1. Generously butter a 9-inch
springform pan. Combine first
3 ingredients; coat bottom of pan
with breadcrumb mixture, and set
aside remaining mixture.
2. Position knife blade in food
processor bowl; add cream cheese.
Process until smooth, stopping
once to scrape down sides. Add
feta cheese, eggs, and sour cream.
Process until smooth, stopping to
scrape down sides. Add artichoke

and next 6 ingredients to processor bowl. Process until smooth,
stopping to scrape down sides.
Pour mixture into prepared pan.
3. Bake, uncovered, at 375°F for
45 to 50 minutes or until lightly
browned. Cool in pan on a wire
rack. Cover and chill 2 hours.
4. Carefully remove sides of springform pan. Pat reserved breadcrumb
mixture on sides of cheesecake.
Serve with toast points or assorted
crackers. Yield: one 9-inch cheesecake (16 appetizer servings).

Quick Creamy Vegetable Dip

Prep: 10 min. • Other: 2 hrs.

$^1/_2$ cup mayonnaise
$^1/_2$ cup sour cream
1 (2-ounce) jar diced pimiento,
    drained
$^1/_4$ cup chopped onion
$^1/_4$ cup diced green bell pepper
$^1/_2$ teaspoon garlic salt
$^1/_8$ teaspoon black pepper
$^1/_8$ teaspoon hot sauce

1. Stir together all ingredients.
Cover and chill 2 hours. Yield:
about 1½ cups.

Balsamic Marinated Olives

Prep: 10 min. • Other: 8½ hrs.

This make-ahead recipe can be easily
halved for a smaller crowd.

2 (6-ounce) jars ripe olives,
    drained
2 (6-ounce) jars kalamata olives,
    drained
2 (7½-ounce) jars pimiento-
    stuffed olives, drained
$^1/_2$ cup olive oil
$^1/_2$ cup balsamic vinegar
1 tablespoon dried Italian
    seasoning

1. Combine all ingredients; cover
and chill at least 8 hours. Let
stand 30 minutes at room temperature before serving. Serve with a
slotted spoon. Yield: 6 cups.

Smoky Baba Ghanoush

DIRECT • MEDIUM
Prep: 10 min. • Cook: 29 min.

2 (1-pound) eggplants, unpeeled
    and cut in half lengthwise
1 garlic clove
$^1/_4$ cup tahini (sesame seed
    paste)
3 tablespoons fresh lemon juice
1 teaspoon salt
6 (6-inch) pita rounds, split
Dash of paprika

1. Grill eggplant over *Direct
Medium* heat 20 minutes or until
very tender, turning occasionally.
Remove eggplant from grill; slightly cool, and peel.
2. Pulse garlic in food processor
4 times or until minced. Add eggplant, tahini, lemon juice, and salt;
process until smooth, stopping to
scrape down sides. Cover and
chill, if desired.
3. When ready to serve, cut each
pita half into 4 wedges; grill over
Direct Medium heat until toasted,
1 to 2 minutes, turning once.
Sprinkle the dip with paprika
and serve with pita wedges. Yield:
12 appetizer servings.

So-Easy Cheese Straws

Prep: 15 min. • Cook: 15 min. • Other: 1 hr.

Cheddar cheese straws are like an old friend you look forward to seeing at a party. And they go quickly, so make plenty.

4 cups (16 ounces) finely shredded sharp Cheddar cheese
¹/₂ cup unsalted butter, softened
2 cups all-purpose flour
1 teaspoon salt
¹/₈ teaspoon ground cayenne pepper

1. Let shredded cheese stand at room temperature 1 hour.
2. Combine cheese and butter in a large mixing bowl; beat at medium speed with an electric mixer until blended.
3. Combine flour, salt, and pepper; add to cheese mixture, beating until dough is no longer crumbly.
4. Roll dough to about ¼-inch thickness on an unfloured surface. Cut into 3- x ½-inch straws. Place 1 inch apart on greased baking sheets. Bake at 350°F for 14 to 15 minutes or until lightly browned. Cool on wire racks. Yield: 11 dozen.

cheese straw variation

For a shapely alternative to the cheese straws above, prepare dough as directed through step 3. Then press dough through a cookie gun fitted with a 1¹/₂- x ¹/₈-inch disk, making long strips of dough 2 inches apart on greased baking sheets. Cut dough crosswise into 3-inch strips. Bake at 350°F for 13 to 14 minutes or until lightly browned. Cool on wire racks. Yield: 7¹/₂ dozen.

Hearty Mint Julep (page 62)

So-Easy Cheese Straws

Layered Nacho Dip

Prep: 15 min.

This quick version of the classic is full of veggies, sour cream, and cheese.

1 (16-ounce) can refried beans
2 teaspoons taco seasoning mix
1 (6-ounce) container avocado dip
1 (8-ounce) container sour cream
1 (4.5-ounce) can chopped ripe olives, drained
2 large tomatoes, diced
1 small onion, diced
1 (4.5-ounce) can chopped green chiles
1¹/₂ cups (6 ounces) shredded Monterey Jack cheese

1. Stir together beans and seasoning mix; spread mixture into an 11- x 7-inch baking dish. Spread avocado dip and sour cream evenly over bean mixture. Sprinkle with olives and next 4 ingredients. Serve with chips. Yield: 8 cups.

Blue Cheese Spread

Prep: 12 min. • Other: 8 hrs.

Three ingredients you probably have on hand make this cheese spread so simple.

1 (8-ounce) package cream cheese, softened
1 (4-ounce) package blue cheese
³/₄ cup finely chopped pecans, toasted and divided

1. Process cream cheese and blue cheese in a food processor 20 seconds or until smooth. Stir in ½ cup chopped pecans.
2. Line a 1½-cup bowl with plastic wrap, and press cream cheese mixture into bowl. Cover and chill at least 8 hours.
3. Unmold cheese; remove plastic wrap. Roll outside edge of cheese mold in remaining ¼ cup chopped pecans. Serve with apple slices and grapes. Yield: 8 to 10 appetizer servings.

Sweet 'n' Savory Snack Mix

Prep: 5 min. • Cook: 12 min.

This party favorite is also the perfect after-school or in-the-car traveling snack.

3 cups crispy corn or rice cereal squares
1 cup small pretzels
1 (6-ounce) can roasted almonds
1 (8-ounce) jar salted peanuts
1/3 cup firmly packed light brown sugar
1 1/2 tablespoons Worcestershire sauce
Vegetable cooking spray
1 cup bear-shaped graham crackers
1/2 cup raisins

1. Combine first 4 ingredients in a large bowl. Stir together brown sugar and Worcestershire sauce until blended; pour over cereal mixture.
2. Spray a 15- x 10-inch jellyroll pan with cooking spray; spread cereal mixture in a single layer in pan, stirring to coat.
3. Bake at 325°F for 12 minutes, stirring every 5 minutes. Stir in graham crackers and raisins. Store in an airtight container. Yield: 8 cups.

Pesto Cream Cheese Mold

Prep: 20 min. • Other: 8 1/2 hrs.

2 (8-ounce) packages cream cheese, softened
1 pound unsalted butter, softened
1/4 cup pine nuts, toasted
2 or 3 garlic cloves
1 cup tightly packed fresh spinach leaves
1 cup tightly packed fresh basil
1/2 cup fresh parsley, stems removed
1/2 teaspoon salt
1/2 cup olive oil
3 cups freshly grated Parmesan cheese (about 3/4 pound)
3 tablespoons unsalted butter, softened
Garnish: fresh parsley sprigs

1. Beat cream cheese and 1 pound butter at medium speed with an electric mixer until smooth; set aside.
2. Process pine nuts, garlic, spinach, basil, parsley, and salt in a food processor until smooth, stopping to scrape down sides. Gradually pour oil through food chute with processor running; process until blended. Add Parmesan cheese and 3 tablespoons butter; process just until blended.
3. Line a 6-cup mold with an 18-inch piece of cheesecloth or heavy-duty plastic wrap, smoothing any wrinkles. Place one-fourth of cream cheese mixture in an even layer in prepared mold; top with one-fourth of pesto mixture. Repeat layers three times, using remaining cream cheese and pesto mixtures. Fold cheesecloth or plastic wrap over top, and pack down lightly. Chill at least 8 hours.
4. About 30 minutes before serving, unfold cheesecloth or plastic wrap, and invert mold onto a serving platter. Carefully peel away cheesecloth or plastic wrap. Garnish platter, if desired. Serve with water crackers or thinly sliced baguettes. Yield: 24 to 30 appetizer servings.

Orange Hummus

Prep: 15 min.

Friends love to break bread together and dipping pita chips in hummus provides the perfect opportunity.

2 (15-ounce) cans chick-peas, drained
1/3 cup orange juice
1/4 cup tahini (sesame seed paste)
1/4 cup olive oil
4 garlic cloves, crushed
1 tablespoon cider vinegar
1 teaspoon soy sauce
1 1/2 teaspoons salt
1/4 teaspoon ground cumin
1/4 teaspoon ground coriander
1/4 teaspoon ground ginger
1/4 teaspoon dry mustard
1/4 teaspoon ground turmeric
1/4 teaspoon paprika
4 green onions, sliced

1. Process first 14 ingredients in a food processor until smooth, stopping to scrape down sides. Stir in green onions. Serve with pita chips. Yield: 3 cups.

Orange Hummus

tropical buzz

Escape to the islands in your own backyard with this sampler of frosty beverages. Kids will love the quenchers on the facing page.

Southern Fruit Punch

Prep: 15 min.

1 (750-milliliter) bottle sweet bourbon, chilled
3/4 cup fresh lemon juice, chilled
1 (12-ounce) can frozen pineapple-orange juice concentrate, thawed and undiluted
1 (2-liter) bottle lemon-lime soft drink, chilled
1 orange, thinly sliced
Garnishes: orange wedges, fresh mint sprigs

1. Stir together first 3 ingredients in a large punch bowl until blended. Stir in soft drink; add orange slices. Garnish, if desired, and serve immediately. Yield: 16 cups.

Piña Colada Slush

Prep: 12 min. • Other: 8 hrs.

1 (46-ounce) can pineapple juice
2 (12-ounce) cans frozen lemonade concentrate, thawed and undiluted
3 cups water
2 cups light rum
1 (15-ounce) can cream of coconut
1 (3-liter) bottle lemon-lime soft drink, chilled
Garnishes: fresh pineapple, fresh flowers

1. Combine first 5 ingredients in a large bowl. Cover and freeze at least 8 hours, stirring twice.
2. To serve, combine equal portions of frozen mixture and soft drink. Serve immediately. Store any remaining frozen mixture in freezer. Garnish, if desired. Yield: 24 cups.

Cranberry Sangría

Prep: 10 min. • Other: 3 hrs.

Get the full-bodied flavor of traditional sangría with just 4 ingredients.

1 (48-ounce) bottle cranberry juice cocktail
3 cups port wine
1 orange, thinly sliced
1 lemon, thinly sliced

1. Combine all ingredients; cover and chill at least 3 hours. Serve over crushed ice. Yield: 6 cups.

Blue Woo-Woo

Prep: 10 min.

1 cup tropical schnapps
1/2 cup blue curaçao
1/4 cup light rum
1 1/2 cups pineapple juice

1. Combine all ingredients and chill. Serve over crushed ice. Yield: 3 1/4 cups.

Mango Margaritas

(pictured on page 4)

Prep: 15 min.

1 (26-ounce) jar sliced mangoes, undrained
Colored decorator sugar
1 (6-ounce) can frozen limeade concentrate, thawed and undiluted
1 cup gold tequila
1/2 cup Triple Sec or Cointreau
1/4 cup Grand Marnier
Crushed ice

1. Spoon 3 tablespoons mango liquid into a saucer; pour sliced mangoes and remaining liquid into an electric blender.
2. Place decorator sugar in a saucer; dip rims of glasses into mango liquid, and then into sugar. Set aside.
3. Add limeade concentrate and next 3 ingredients to blender; process until smooth, stopping to scrape down sides. Pour half of mixture into a pitcher; set aside.
4. Add enough ice to remaining mixture in blender to bring mixture to 5-cup level; process until slushy, stopping to scrape down sides. Pour into prepared glasses; repeat with remaining mango mixture and ice. Serve immediately. Yield: 10 cups.

Hearty Mint Juleps

Prep: 12 min. • Cook: 5 min. • Other: 13 hrs.

This potent beverage (photo, page 60) became the official drink of the Kentucky Derby in 1875, but it's just as refreshing in your own backyard.

2 1/4 cups sugar
1 cup water
1/2 cup packed fresh mint leaves
2 cups bourbon
Garnish: fresh mint sprigs

1. Combine first 3 ingredients in a medium saucepan. Bring to a boil; boil, stirring constantly, 5 minutes or until sugar dissolves. Remove from heat. Let stand 12 hours at room temperature, stirring occasionally.
2. Pour liquid through a wire-mesh strainer into a pitcher, discarding mint. Stir in bourbon; chill. Serve over crushed ice. Garnish, if desired. Yield: 3 1/2 cups.

Sunshine Fizz

Prep: 4 min.

1 cup pineapple juice, chilled
1 cup orange juice, chilled
1 cup orange sherbet
1/2 cup club soda, chilled
Orange sherbet

1. Process pineapple juice, orange juice, and 1 cup sherbet in a blender until smooth, stopping to scrape down sides. Stir in club soda, and pour into soda glasses. Add 1/4 cup scoop of orange sherbet to each glass, and serve immediately. Yield: 4 cups.

Old-Fashioned Lemonade

Prep: 10 min.

1 1/2 cups sugar
1/2 cup boiling water
1 1/2 cups fresh lemon juice (6 to 8 large lemons)
5 cups cold water
Garnishes: lemon slices, fresh mint sprigs

1. Stir together sugar and 1/2 cup boiling water until sugar dissolves. Stir in lemon juice and 5 cups cold water. Garnish, if desired. Yield: 8 cups.

Berry Good Punch

Prep: 4 min.

1 (10-ounce) package frozen strawberries in syrup, thawed
1 (12-ounce) can frozen cranberry juice cocktail concentrate, thawed and undiluted
1 (12-ounce) can frozen lemonade concentrate, thawed and undiluted
2 (1-liter) bottles club soda, chilled
1 (1-liter) bottle ginger ale, chilled

1. Process berries in a blender until smooth. Pour into a punch bowl; add cranberry juice and remaining ingredients. Yield: 13 cups.

Cranberry Sangría

Southern Fruit Punch

Blue Woo-Woo

Piña Colada Slush

mouthwatering meats

From smoky brisket to succulent tenderloin, there's something for every meat-lover within these pages.

Pork Medaillons with Blackberry Sauce

DIRECT • MEDIUM

Prep: 10 min. • Cook: 40 min. • Other: 40 min.

2 (1-pound) pork tenderloins
1 teaspoon salt
1 teaspoon coarsely ground black pepper
1 teaspoon coarsely ground whole allspice
¼ cup unsalted butter, divided
3 large shallots, finely chopped
⅔ cup dry white wine
3 tablespoons seedless blackberry fruit spread
Garnishes: fresh blackberries, fresh thyme sprigs

1. Sprinkle pork evenly with salt, pepper, and allspice. Allow to stand at room temperature 20 to 30 minutes before grilling.
2. Grill pork over *Direct Medium* heat until the centers are barely pink and the internal temperature registers 150°F, 15 to 20 minutes, turning pork every 5 minutes. Let rest for 3 to 5 minutes.
3. Meanwhile, melt 2 tablespoons butter in a small saucepan over medium-high heat. Add shallots, and sauté 5 minutes or until tender. Add wine; cook 13 minutes or until liquid is reduced by half. Reduce heat to low; whisk in fruit spread and remaining 2 tablespoons butter. Cook 2 minutes or until slightly thickened. Cut pork into ¼-inch-thick slices. Drizzle blackberry sauce over pork. Garnish, if desired. Yield: 6 servings.

Molasses-Grilled Chops with Horseradish Sauce

DIRECT • MEDIUM

Prep: 8 min. • Cook: 10 min. • Other: 8 hrs.

Spray the measuring cup with vegetable cooking spray or rinse it in cold water before measuring sticky molasses. The molasses will slide right out of the cup.

4 (4-ounce) boneless center-cut loin pork chops (½ inch thick)
½ cup soy sauce
¼ cup molasses
1 teaspoon garlic powder
¼ cup mayonnaise
3 tablespoons milk
1 tablespoon prepared horseradish
2 teaspoons finely chopped white onion
¼ teaspoon ground black pepper

1. Place pork chops in a large zip-top freezer bag. Combine soy sauce, molasses, and garlic powder; stir well, and pour over chops. Seal bag; turn bag to coat chops. Marinate in refrigerator 4 to 8 hours, turning occasionally.
2. Remove pork chops from marinade, discarding marinade. Grill pork over *Direct Medium* heat until the juices run clear, 6 to 8 minutes, turning once. Let rest for 5 minutes.
3. Meanwhile, combine mayonnaise and remaining 4 ingredients in a small saucepan. Cook over low heat, stirring constantly, until thoroughly heated. Spoon horseradish sauce evenly over chops. Yield: 4 servings.

Pork Medaillons with Blackberry Sauce

Molasses-Grilled Chops with
Horseradish Sauce

Pork Tacos with Pineapple Salsa

DIRECT • MEDIUM

Prep: 10 min. • Cook: 8 min. • Other: 25 min.

1 tablespoon curry powder
$1/2$ teaspoon garlic powder
$1/4$ teaspoon salt
$1/4$ teaspoon freshly ground black pepper
$1/8$ teaspoon ground cayenne pepper
6 (4-ounce) boneless pork loin chops ($1/2$ inch thick)
Extra-virgin olive oil
Pineapple Salsa
8 (8-inch) flour tortillas, warmed

1. Combine first 5 ingredients; sprinkle over pork chops. Brush or spray chops with oil. Allow to stand at room temperature 20 to 30 minutes before grilling.
2. Grill over *Direct Medium* heat until the juices run clear, 6 to 8 minutes, turning once. Let rest 5 minutes. Coarsely chop pork. Serve with Pineapple Salsa and warm tortillas. Yield: 8 servings.

Pineapple Salsa

Prep: 12 min.

$1/4$ cup fresh orange juice
2 tablespoons fresh lemon juice
1 tablespoon honey
$1/4$ teaspoon salt
$1/4$ teaspoon ground black pepper
2 cups finely chopped fresh pineapple
2 tablespoons finely chopped fresh cilantro
$1/4$ small red onion, finely chopped

1. Whisk together first 5 ingredients. Stir in pineapple, cilantro, and onion. Yield: 2 cups.

The fruited salsa and peppered pork present a sweet-hot play on flavors.

Cajun Grilled Tenderloin

SEAR: MEDIUM

GRILL: INDIRECT • MEDIUM

Prep: 15 min. • Cook: 35 min. • Other: 2 hrs.

1 ($3^{1}/2$-pound) beef tenderloin
$1/4$ cup hot sauce
$1/4$ cup teriyaki sauce
2 tablespoons Worcestershire sauce
1 tablespoon Creole seasoning
Cocktail buns
Mustard-Horseradish Cream

1. Place tenderloin in a large zip-top freezer bag. Combine hot sauce and next 3 ingredients. Pour over tenderloin. Seal bag; marinate in refrigerator $1^{1}/2$ hours, turning occasionally.
2. Remove tenderloin from marinade, discarding marinade. Allow tenderloin to stand at room temperature 30 minutes before grilling.
3. Grill tenderloin over *Direct Medium* heat 15 minutes, turning every 5 minutes. Continue grilling over *Indirect Medium* heat until the internal temperature reaches 135°F for medium-rare, 15 to 20 minutes. Remove tenderloin from grill and let rest at least 10 minutes before slicing. Serve on buns with Mustard-Horseradish Cream. Yield: 24 cocktail sandwiches or 8 entrée servings.

Mustard-Horseradish Cream

Prep: 10 min. • Other: 30 min.

$1/4$ cup prepared horseradish
1 cup whipping cream
$1/4$ cup Dijon mustard
1 tablespoon fresh lemon juice

1. Place horseradish in a fine wire-mesh strainer; press with back of a spoon against sides of strainer to squeeze out juice. Discard juice. Set horseradish aside.
2. Beat whipping cream at high speed with an electric mixer until soft peaks form. Fold in horseradish, mustard, and lemon juice. Cover and chill. Yield: $2^{1}/2$ cups.

Beef Fajitas

DIRECT • HIGH

Prep: 20 min. • Cook: 20 min. • Other: $8^{1}/2$ hrs.

2 (1-pound) skirt steaks
$1/3$ cup fresh lime juice
$1/3$ cup olive oil
4 large garlic cloves, minced
$1^{1}/2$ teaspoons ground cumin
2 teaspoons cracked black pepper
1 large white onion, cut crosswise into $1/3$-inch slices
Salt and pepper to taste
8 (8-inch) flour tortillas
Assorted toppings (optional)

1. Place steaks between 2 sheets of heavy-duty plastic wrap; gently pound to an even thickness, using a meat mallet or rolling pin. Place steaks in a zip-top freezer bag or large shallow dish.
2. Combine lime juice and next 4 ingredients, stirring well. Pour marinade over meat. Seal or cover, and marinate in refrigerator 8 hours, turning meat occasionally.
3. Remove steaks from marinade, reserving marinade. Allow steaks to stand at room temperature for 20 to 30 minutes before grilling. Pour the marinade into a small saucepan, bring to a boil, and boil for 1 full minute; set aside. Grill steaks over *Direct High* heat until cooked to desired doneness, 4 to 6 minutes for medium-rare, turning once and basting with marinade.
4. Meanwhile, lightly brush onions with boiled marinade and season with salt and pepper to taste. Grill over *Direct High* heat until tender, about 6 minutes.
5. Wrap tortillas in aluminum foil and grill over *Indirect High* heat until thoroughly heated, about 8 minutes, turning tortillas occasionally.
6. Slice steaks diagonally across the grain into thin slices. Divide meat and onion evenly among tortillas. Top each serving with desired toppings, such as chopped tomato, sour cream, or shredded lettuce. Roll up tortillas. Yield: 8 servings.

Smoked Brisket

Smoked Brisket

INDIRECT • LOW
Prep: 15 min. • Cook: 7 hrs. • Other: 45 min.

2 tablespoons dried rosemary
2 tablespoons paprika
2 tablespoons freshly ground
    black pepper
2 tablespoons dried garlic flakes
1 teaspoon salt
1 (7-pound) untrimmed, center-cut
    beef brisket
Olive oil
Hickory wood chips, soaked in
    water for at least 30 minutes
Barbecue sauce
Hamburger buns
Garnish: fresh rosemary sprigs

1. Combine first 5 ingredients; rub on brisket. Brush or spray the brisket with oil. Allow brisket to stand at room temperature for 20 to 30 minutes before grilling.
2. Follow the grill's instructions for using wood chips. Grill brisket, fat side up, over *Indirect Low* heat until golden brown, about 3½ hours, keeping the grill temperature about 300°F. The internal temperature should reach 165°F.
3. Brush brisket with barbecue sauce and wrap in heavy-duty aluminum foil. Continue to grill over *Indirect Low* heat until very tender, about 3½ hours more. The internal temperature should reach 190°F.
4. Remove from grill and let rest for about 15 minutes. Unwrap brisket. Slice and serve with barbecue sauce and buns. Garnish, if desired. Yield: 8 servings.

Lamb Chops with Mint Marinade

DIRECT • MEDIUM
Prep: 10 min. • Cook: 10 min. • Other: 8½ hrs.

Tangy-sweet hoisin sauce punches up the flavor in this marinade that's also good with beef or pork. Save the remaining sauce in the refrigerator and use it instead of ketchup.

6 lamb sirloin chops
    (1 inch thick)
¹⁄₃ cup molasses
¹⁄₄ cup minced fresh spearmint
1 tablespoon peeled, grated
    ginger
3 tablespoons soy sauce
3 tablespoons hoisin sauce
2 tablespoons water
2 garlic cloves, minced

1. Place lamb chops in a zip-top freezer bag or shallow dish. Combine molasses and next 6 ingredients; stir well. Pour half of mixture over chops. Seal or cover, and marinate in refrigerator 8 hours. Cover and chill remaining marinade.
2. Remove chops from marinade, discarding marinade in the bag or dish. Allow chops to stand at room temperature for 20 to 30 minutes before grilling. Grill chops over *Direct Medium* heat until medium-rare, 10 minutes, turning once and basting often with reserved marinade. Yield: 6 servings.

the pleasures of planking

Plank cooking is so simple it's almost foolproof. Unlike grilled foods, which can dry out quickly when left on the grill too long, food cooked on a plank stays moist and tender because of the damp smoke that wafts from the wood plank. The smoldering plank adds a smoky essence that complements other flavors without overpowering them. Everything from tuna to tenderloin can be prepared and served on a plank.

Wood Choices

Planks suited for grilling are widely available, conveniently packaged, and sized to fit standard grills. The subtle flavors of different woods are difficult to distinguish, especially when sassy sauces and side dishes accompany the entrée. Alder and cedar planks are the easiest to find.

Alder produces a delicate flavor that works well with mild foods. It's a good match for seafood—especially salmon. Cedar, the most aromatic wood, adds a deep but gentle flavor that resembles its familiar aroma. It also stands up nicely to spicy dishes. Pair cedar with hearty foods, such as pork. Hickory gives an intense smoky flavor that works well with beef and chicken (think of barbecue and spicy rubs and sauces). Oak imparts a moderate flavor that blends well with a variety of meats, poultry, and fish. Resinous woods, such as birch, pine, and poplar, impart a bitter flavor, so avoid them.

Planking Pointers

- Soak planks before using to help keep the meat moist. A soaked plank produces maximum smoke and is less likely to burn. Submerge it in water at least an hour (see photo 1, below).
- Use the soaked plank right away since the wood will start to dry out quickly.
- After placing the plank on the grill, immediately cover the grill so that smoke quickly surrounds the food.
- Food that touches the wood takes on more flavor, so arrange it on the wood plank in a single layer (see photo 2, below).
- Use oven mitts to remove the plank and place it on a heatproof serving platter or baking sheet. The edges of the plank may be charred and smoldering.

Argentinean Oak-Planked Beef Tenderloin with Chimichurri Sauce

DIRECT • MEDIUM
Prep: 15 min. • Cook: 17 min. • Other: 1 hr.

The sauce, made from fresh herbs, is a robust accompaniment with the simple tenderloin.

1 (15- x 6$^1/_2$- x $^3/_8$-inch) untreated
   oak grilling plank
4 (4-ounce) beef tenderloin
   steaks ($^3/_4$ inch thick)
$^1/_2$ teaspoon salt
$^1/_4$ teaspoon freshly ground
   black pepper
$^3/_4$ cup fresh flat-leaf parsley
   leaves
$^1/_4$ cup fresh cilantro leaves
$^1/_4$ cup fresh mint leaves
$^1/_4$ cup chopped onion
$^1/_4$ cup chicken broth
3 tablespoons sherry vinegar
2 tablespoons fresh oregano
   leaves
1 teaspoon olive oil
$^1/_2$ teaspoon salt
$^1/_2$ teaspoon freshly ground
   black pepper
$^1/_2$ teaspoon dried crushed red
   pepper
3 garlic cloves

1. Submerge plank in water 1 hour or longer; drain.
2. Sprinkle steaks evenly with salt and black pepper. Allow to stand at room temperature 20 to 30 minutes before grilling.
3. Grill plank over *Direct Medium* heat until lightly charred, about 5 minutes. Carefully turn plank over. Place steaks on charred side of plank. Grill steaks over *Direct Medium* heat until the meat is medium-rare, about 12 minutes.
4. To prepare sauce, combine parsley and remaining ingredients in a food processor, and process until smooth. Serve with steaks. Yield: 4 servings.

**Argentinean Oak-Planked Beef
Tenderloin with Chimichurri Sauce**

sensational chicken choices

From slow-smoked to quick grilled, the grill offers lots of sizzling supper options for the poultry family.

Beer Can Chicken

INDIRECT • MEDIUM
Prep: 10 min. • Cook: 1 hr., 20 min.
Other: 8 hrs., 10 min.

If you need extra time to set up your serving table, keep the chicken warm in the oven at about 200°F while you finish up.

3 (3- to 4-pound) whole chickens
4 (12-ounce) cans beer, divided
1 (8-ounce) bottle Italian dressing
1/4 to 1/3 cup fajita seasoning

1. Place each chicken in a large zip-top freezer bag.
2. Combine 1 can beer, Italian dressing, and fajita seasoning; pour evenly over chickens. Seal bags, and chill 8 hours, turning occasionally.
3. Remove chicken from marinade, discarding marinade in the bag.
4. Open remaining 3 cans beer and pour out about half the beer in each can. Place each chicken upright onto a beer can, fitting

into cavity. Pull legs forward to form a tripod, allowing chickens to stand upright.
5. Place chickens upright on the cooking grate. Grill the chickens over *Indirect Medium* heat until the juices run clear and the internal temperature reaches 170°F in the breast and 180°F in the thickest part of the thigh, 1 hour and 20 minutes. Remove the chicken from the grill and let rest for about 10 minutes. Carefully remove cans, and cut chickens into quarters. Yield: 12 servings.

A tomato-basil vinaigrette doubles as a marinade and a finishing sauce for tender grilled chicken breasts.

---

try a poultry roaster

Rather than using a beer can for Beer Can Chicken (above), consider using a poultry roaster instead. Not only is a poultry roaster ideal for infusing the chicken with the subtle flavor of your favorite beer, it's also cleaner and reusable. Look for poultry roasters at large hardware stores or wherever grills are sold.

Grilled Tomato-Basil Chicken

DIRECT • MEDIUM-HIGH
Prep: 15 min. • Cook: 10 min. • Other: 8 hrs.

1 garlic clove, halved
4 plum tomatoes, quartered
3/4 cup balsamic vinegar
1/4 cup fresh basil leaves
1/2 teaspoon ground black pepper
1/4 teaspoon salt
4 (4-ounce) skinned and boned chicken breasts
4 plum tomatoes, halved
Extra-virgin olive oil

1. Combine first 6 ingredients in food processor bowl. Process until smooth. Set aside 1/4 cup tomato mixture.
2. Place chicken in a large zip-top freezer bag. Pour remaining tomato mixture over chicken. Seal bag; turn bag to coat chicken. Marinate in refrigerator 8 hours.
3. Remove chicken from marinade, discarding marinade in the bag. Lightly brush or spray tomato halves with oil. Place chicken and tomato halves on the cooking grate. Grill over *Direct Medium-High* heat until tomato is cooked but still slightly firm and chicken is firm and juices run clear, 8 to 10 minutes, turning tomato and chicken once.
4. Place chicken on 4 individual serving plates; top each chicken breast with 1 tablespoon reserved tomato mixture. Arrange 2 grilled tomato halves on each plate with chicken. Yield: 4 servings.

Grilled Tomato-Basil Chicken

Maple-Mustard Grilled Chicken

INDIRECT • MEDIUM
Prep: 4 min. • Cook: 40 min.

This simple recipe highlights the favorite flavor combination of sweet with tangy.

$1/2$ cup Dijon mustard
$1/4$ cup maple syrup
2 tablespoons white vinegar
4 (6-ounce) bone-in chicken breasts
$1/2$ teaspoon ground black pepper
$1/8$ teaspoon salt
Extra-virgin olive oil

1. Combine first 3 ingredients in a small bowl, stirring well; set aside.
2. Sprinkle chicken with pepper and salt. Lightly brush or spray chicken with oil.
3. Grill chicken, skin side up, over *Indirect Medium* heat until firm and the juices run clear, 30 to 40 minutes, basting with mustard mixture during the last 15 minutes of grilling time. Yield: 4 servings.

Mesquite-Smoked Turkey Breast

INDIRECT • MEDIUM-HIGH
Prep: 10 min. • Cook: 3 hrs. • Other: 50 min.

$1/4$ cup Mexican Seasoning Blend
1 (6-pound) bone-in turkey breast, skinned
Extra-virgin olive oil
Mesquite chips, soaked in water for at least 30 minutes

1. Rub Mexican Seasoning Blend inside and outside turkey breast. Lightly brush or spray turkey breast with oil.
2. Follow the grill's instructions for using wood chips. Grill the turkey breast, bone side down, over *Indirect Medium-High* heat until the internal temperature reaches 170°F, 2 to 3 hours. Let rest for 20 minutes before slicing. Yield: 12 servings.

Mexican Seasoning Blend

Prep: 5 min.

$1/4$ cup prepared chili powder
2 tablespoons paprika
1 tablespoon ground cumin
1 teaspoon granulated garlic
1 teaspoon salt
$1/2$ teaspoon ground cayenne pepper

1. Combine all ingredients in a small bowl. Store in an airtight container; shake well before each use. Yield: 1 cup.

Lemon-Dijon Rotisserie Chicken

INDIRECT • MEDIUM
Prep: 15 min. • Cook: $1 1/4$ hrs. • Other: 10 min.

2 teaspoons Dijon mustard
2 teaspoons fresh lemon juice
2 teaspoons olive oil
1 teaspoon paprika
1 teaspoon granulated onion
$3/4$ teaspoon kosher salt
$1/2$ teaspoon ground cumin
$1/2$ teaspoon freshly ground black pepper
1 whole chicken (4 to $4 1/2$ pounds)

1. Whisk together the first 8 ingredients in a medium bowl.
2. Remove the wing tips, giblets, and excess fat from the chicken. Spread the glaze evenly on the outside of the chicken. Stuff the squeezed lemon inside the chicken. Truss the chicken with kitchen string.
3. Following the grill's instructions, secure the chicken in the middle of a rotisserie spit, put the rotisserie spit in place, and turn the rotisserie on. Cook the chicken over *Indirect Medium* heat, keeping the grill temperature between 350°F and 400°F, until the internal temperature registers 180°F in the thickest part of the thigh and the juices run clear, 1 to $1 1/4$ hours.
4. When the chicken is fully cooked, turn off the rotisserie and, using thick barbecue mitts, remove the rotisserie spit from the grill.

Slide the chicken from the rotisserie spit onto a cutting board. Let the chicken rest for 5 to 10 minutes before carving into serving pieces. Serve warm. Yield: 4 servings.

Asian Grilled Cornish Hens

INDIRECT • MEDIUM-HIGH
Prep: 15 min. • Cook: 1 hr. • Other: 30 min.

$1/4$ cup hoisin sauce
2 tablespoons sesame seeds
3 tablespoons chile-garlic sauce
3 tablespoons dark sesame oil
3 tablespoons honey
1 teaspoon ground ginger
4 (1- to $1 1/2$-pound) Cornish hens
1 (14-ounce) can chicken broth
2 teaspoons cornstarch
Garnish: thinly sliced green onions or green onion curls

1. Combine first 6 ingredients in a shallow dish or large zip-top freezer bag, gently squeezing to blend; add Cornish hens. Cover or seal, and chill 30 minutes, turning occasionally.
2. Remove Cornish hens from marinade, reserving marinade.
3. Grill hens, breast side down, over *Indirect Medium-High* heat until the juices run clear and meat is no longer pink at the bone, 30 to 45 minutes. Remove from the grill and let rest while making the sauce.
4. Pour marinade into a small saucepan. Reserve $1/4$ cup chicken broth, and add remaining broth to marinade. Bring marinade mixture to a boil over medium-high heat and boil for 5 minutes. Whisk together cornstarch and reserved $1/4$ cup chicken broth until smooth. Whisk into marinade mixture; boil, whisking constantly, about 1 minute. Serve with Cornish hens, and garnish, if desired. Yield: 4 servings.

Marinated Chicken Quarters

INDIRECT • MEDIUM
Prep: 15 min. • Cook: 50 min. • Other: 8 hrs.

$^1/_2$ cup unsalted butter, melted
$^1/_2$ cup fresh lemon juice
1 tablespoon paprika
1 tablespoon dried oregano
1 teaspoon garlic salt
1 teaspoon dried or 1 tablespoon chopped fresh cilantro
1 teaspoon ground cumin
1 (3-pound) whole chicken, quartered
$^1/_2$ teaspoon salt
$^1/_2$ teaspoon black pepper

1. Combine first 7 ingredients; reserve $^1/_2$ cup butter mixture.
2. Sprinkle chicken evenly with salt and pepper. Place in shallow dishes or zip-top freezer bags; pour remaining butter mixture evenly over chicken. Cover or seal, and chill, along with reserved butter mixture, for 8 hours, turning occasionally.
3. Remove chicken from marinade, discarding marinade in the dish or bag.
4. Grill, skin side up, over *Indirect Medium* heat until juices run clear and internal temperature reaches 170°F in the breast and 180°F in the thickest part of the thigh, 40 to 50 minutes, basting with reserved butter mixture during the last 15 minutes of grilling time. Yield: 4 servings.

Note: Bone-in breast halves can be used in place of the chicken quarters.

menu on the grill

For an all-on-the-grill meal, pair Marinated Chicken Quarters with Easy Vegetable Kabobs (page 94). Let the chicken cook about 20 minutes before adding the kabobs to the grill.

Marinated Chicken Quarters

seafood sizzle

Fish and shellfish soak up great grilled flavor in these quick-cooking entrées.

Grilled Salmon with Nectarine-Onion Relish

DIRECT • HIGH
Prep: 5 min. • Cook: 11 min.

4 (6-ounce) salmon fillets (about 1 inch thick)
$1/2$ teaspoon salt
$1/2$ teaspoon freshly ground black pepper
Extra-virgin olive oil
Nectarine-Onion Relish

1. Sprinkle salmon fillets with salt and pepper and lightly brush or spray both sides with oil.
2. Grill salmon fillets, flesh side down, over *Direct High* heat until you can lift the fillets with tongs without their sticking to the grate, 7 to 8 minutes. Turn, skin side down, and finish cooking for 2 to 3 minutes more. Slide a spatula between the skin and flesh and transfer fillets to serving plates. Serve hot with Nectarine-Onion Relish. Yield: 4 servings.

Nectarine-Onion Relish

Prep: 10 min. • Other: 2 hrs.

3 medium nectarines, medium diced
1 large red bell pepper, medium diced
1 medium red onion, medium diced
$1/4$ cup thinly sliced fresh basil
$1/4$ cup white wine vinegar
$1/2$ teaspoon grated orange zest
$1/4$ cup fresh orange juice
2 jalapeño peppers, seeded and minced
2 tablespoons fresh lime juice
2 teaspoons granulated sugar
2 garlic cloves, minced
$1/4$ teaspoon salt

1. Stir together all ingredients. Cover and chill 2 hours. Yield: about 4 cups.

Grilled Grouper with Apricot-Ginger Relish

DIRECT • HIGH
Prep: 15 min. • Cook: 6 min. • Other: 1 hr.

Fresh apricots are highly perishable. You can store them in the fridge for up to 2 days, or use them as soon as you buy them.

2 cups medium-diced fresh apricots (about 6 medium)
$1/2$ cup medium-diced red bell pepper
$1/3$ cup rice wine vinegar
$1/4$ cup minced green onions
2 tablespoons minced peeled fresh ginger
$1/2$ teaspoon freshly ground black pepper
$1/4$ teaspoon salt
$1/4$ teaspoon hot sauce
1 tablespoon chile paste with garlic
4 (6-ounce) grouper fillets ($1/2$ inch thick)
Extra-virgin olive oil

1. Combine the first 8 ingredients in a bowl, and stir until blended. Let relish stand for 1 hour.
2. Rub the chile paste over both sides of the grouper fillets. Brush or spray both sides of fillets with olive oil. Grill the fillets over *Direct High* heat until just turning opaque in the center, 5 to 6 minutes, turning once. Serve warm with apricot-ginger relish. Yield: 4 servings.

Grilled Swordfish with Caper Sauce

DIRECT • HIGH
Prep: 15 min. • Cook: 8 min. • Other: 1 hr.

$1/2$ cup dry white wine
5 garlic cloves, minced
2 teaspoons finely chopped fresh rosemary, divided
$1/4$ teaspoon salt
$1/4$ teaspoon black pepper
4 (4-ounce) swordfish steaks ($3/4$ inch thick)
Extra-virgin olive oil
$1/3$ cup fresh lemon juice
3 tablespoons basil olive oil or olive oil
1 tablespoon capers
3 tablespoons fine, dry breadcrumbs
Garnish: fresh rosemary sprigs

1. Combine wine, garlic, and 1 teaspoon rosemary in an 8-inch square baking dish.
2. Sprinkle salt and pepper over fish; place fish in baking dish, turning to coat. Cover and chill at least 1 hour. Remove fish, discarding marinade. Lightly brush or spray fish with oil.
3. Grill the fish over *Direct High* heat until just turning opaque in the center, 6 to 8 minutes, turning once.
4. Combine remaining 1 teaspoon rosemary, lemon juice, and next 3 ingredients. Spoon over fish, and garnish, if desired. Serve immediately. Yield: 4 servings.

Grilled Swordfish
with Caper Sauce

Citrus-Marinated
Smoked Shrimp

Citrus-Marinated Smoked Shrimp

DIRECT • HIGH

Prep: 15 min. • Cook: 11 min. • Other: 1 hr.

2 pounds unpeeled, jumbo shrimp
1 cup fresh orange juice
1/4 cup honey
1 teaspoon grated orange zest
1 tablespoon finely chopped fresh basil
1 tablespoon finely chopped fresh thyme
Maple or cherry wood chunks, soaked in water for at least 30 minutes
Extra-virgin olive oil
Salt
Freshly ground black pepper
Garnishes: orange slices, fresh thyme sprigs

1. Place shrimp in a shallow dish or large zip-top freezer bag. Stir together orange juice and next 4 ingredients; pour over shrimp, stirring to coat. Cover or seal, and chill 1 hour. Drain, reserving marinade. Pour marinade into a small saucepan. Bring to a boil, reduce heat, and simmer, uncovered, 5 to 7 minutes or until reduced by half.
2. Follow the grill's instructions for using wood chunks. Lightly brush or spray shrimp with oil. Season with salt and pepper. Grill over *Direct High* heat until shrimp are just opaque in the center and firm to the touch, 2 to 4 minutes, turning once. Remove from the grill and serve with reduced marinade. Garnish, if desired. Yield: 3 to 4 servings.

Maple-Glazed Scallops

DIRECT • MEDIUM-HIGH

Prep: 20 min. • Cook: 17 min.

12 bacon slices, cut in half
24 large sea scallops (about 2 pounds)
1 cup maple syrup
2 tablespoons unsalted butter, melted
1 teaspoon grated orange zest
3 tablespoons fresh orange juice
1/8 teaspoon salt
Garnish: orange wedges

1. Cook bacon in a very large skillet over medium heat for 5 to 6 minutes. Cut bacon slices in half again so each one is 3 to 4 inches long. Wrap each scallop with a piece of bacon. Set aside.
2. Bring syrup to a boil in a saucepan over medium-high heat. Cook, uncovered, until reduced to 2/3 cup, about 5 minutes. Remove from heat; stir in butter and next 3 ingredients.
3. Thread 4 bacon-wrapped scallops on each of 6 kabobs, using 2 (10- to 12-inch) skewers for each kabob to keep scallops from rotating; brush syrup mixture over kabobs. Grill kabobs over *Direct Medium-High* heat until just opaque in the center and bacon is crisp, 4 to 6 minutes, turning once or twice. Garnish, if desired. Yield: 6 servings.

Easy Roasted Oysters

DIRECT • HIGH

Prep: 10 min. • Cook: 9 min.

About 5 dozen oysters in the shell
A sheet of tin cut 1 inch smaller than the size of the grill
A double thickness of burlap (large enough to cover oysters)
A spray bottle (to mist burlap)
Spicy Cocktail Sauce
Melted butter
Hot sauce
Saltine crackers

1. Arrange oysters in the shell on a sheet of tin on the cooking grate; cover with burlap, but don't let burlap fall over the edges of the tin. Mist burlap generously with water, and grill oysters over *Direct High* heat 7 to 9 minutes.
2. Uncover oysters and remove from the grill with long-handled tongs. Open and serve with Spicy Cocktail Sauce, melted butter, hot sauce, and saltine crackers. Yield: 2 servings.

Spicy Cocktail Sauce

Prep: 7 min.

2 cups ketchup
3/4 cup chili sauce
1/2 cup prepared horseradish
1/4 cup red wine vinegar
2 tablespoons Worcestershire sauce
1 tablespoon fresh lemon juice
2 tablespoons minced yellow onion
2 tablespoons minced celery
1 teaspoon freshly ground black pepper

1. Combine all ingredients in a small bowl, stirring until blended; cover and chill. Yield: 4 cups.

Maple-Glazed Scallops

barbecue hall of flame

Master the time-honored art of barbecue, be it smoke-infused, slow-cooked, slathered with spicy sauces, or all of the above. Not much is more enjoyable than fall-off-the-bone, tender barbecued meat, and these foolproof recipes prove it.

Smoky Chipotle Baby Back Ribs

INDIRECT • MEDIUM
Prep: 15 min. • Cook: 2 hrs. • Other: 8¹/₂ hrs.

These ribs have all-day flavor but take less than 3 hours to cook.

3 slabs baby back pork ribs
  (about 5¹/₂ pounds)
2 oranges, halved
Chipotle Rub (page 84)
Smoky Chipotle 'Cue Sauce
  (page 83)

1. Remove the thin membrane from the back of ribs by slicing into it with a knife and then pulling it off (this will make ribs more tender).
2. Rub the oranges, squeezing as you rub, all over the meat. Massage Chipotle Rub into meat, covering all sides. Wrap tightly with plastic wrap, and place in a zip-top freezer bag or 13- x 9-inch dish; chill 8 hours. Let ribs stand at room temperature 30 minutes

before grilling. Remove plastic wrap. Place ribs in rib rack.
3. Grill over *Indirect Medium* heat for 2 hours, basting with half of the Smoky Chipotle 'Cue Sauce the last 30 minutes of grilling. Remove ribs from grill and let rest 10 minutes. Cut ribs, slicing between bones. Serve with remaining sauce. Yield: 6 servings.

---

our best tips for grilling ribs

Here are our best tips for grilling ribs using the Smoky Chipotle Baby Back Ribs recipe.

• Don't skip rubbing the ribs with orange halves; the juice adds a perky zip to the flavor.
• Remove the thin membrane on the back, or bone side, of each rib rack to make the cooked meat almost fall off the bone. Removing the membrane also allows the seasonings and sauces to better penetrate the meat.
• For best flavor, wrap seasoned ribs in plastic wrap to hold rub mixture close to the meat. Place each slab in a separate 2-gallon zip-top freezer bag, and refrigerate overnight. When ready to grill, unwrapping the ribs can be messy, so hang a zip-top freezer bag on the grill handle, being careful that it doesn't touch the hot grill. Unwrap ribs over the bag, discarding plastic wrap into bag. Slide ribs into rib rack (photo 1). Immediately remove bag from handle and discard. Ribs also can be placed directly on the food grate; however, expect to turn the ribs and manage the fire more often. To maintain temperature, stoke the fire, and make sure vents are open.
• When the meat is tender and done, bones should wiggle easily when moved, and the meat will be shrunk down from the bones. Slow the fire before basting by partially or fully closing vents. Pour sauce over ribs, guiding it to cover with a grill brush (photo 2).

Smoky Chipotle
Baby Back Ribs

Barbecue Pork
Sandwiches

Barbecue Pork Sandwiches

INDIRECT • MEDIUM
Prep: 20 min. • Cook: 6 hrs. • Other: 8^1/$_2$ hrs.

1 (10-ounce) bottle teriyaki sauce
1 cup honey
^{1}/$_2$ cup cider vinegar
2 tablespoons black pepper
2 tablespoons garlic powder
1 teaspoon dried crushed red
    pepper
1 (6-pound) bone-in Boston butt
    pork roast
Hickory wood chunks, soaked in
    water for at least 30 minutes
Tangy Barbecue Sauce (page 83)
Hamburger buns
Dill pickle slices

1. Combine first 6 ingredients in a
shallow dish or large zip-top freezer bag. Cut deep slits in roast using
a paring knife; add roast to marinade. Cover or seal, and chill 8
hours, turning occasionally.
2. Follow the grill's or smoker's
instructions for using wood chunks.
If using a grill, place roast over
Indirect Medium heat. If using a
smoker, place water pan in smoker,
add water to depth of fill line, and
place roast in center of lower food
rack.
3. Grill or smoke over *Indirect
Medium* heat until the internal
temperature reaches about 190°F,
about 6 hours, adding additional
water, if necessary. Remove from
grill or smoker; cool slightly. Chop
or shred pork; stir 2 to 3 cups hot
Tangy Barbecue Sauce into shredded pork. Serve on buns with additional barbecue sauce and pickle
slices. Yield: 10 to 12 servings.

Lone Star Barbecue Beef

INDIRECT • LOW
Prep: 15 min. • Cook: 5 hrs. • Other: 8 hrs.

1 cup vegetable oil
1 cup cider vinegar
^{1}/$_4$ cup Worcestershire sauce
1 bay leaf, crumbled
1^1/$_4$ teaspoons seasoned salt
2^1/$_4$ teaspoons ground black
    pepper
^{3}/$_4$ teaspoon paprika
1 (3-pound) beef brisket,
    trimmed
Oak or hickory chunks, soaked in
    water for at least 30 minutes
Texas Barbecue Sauce (page 84)

Serve these sandwiches
with your favorite baked
beans recipe.

1. Combine first 4 ingredients in
a shallow dish or large zip-top
freezer bag.
2. Combine seasoned salt, pepper,
and paprika; rub all over the
brisket. Place brisket in marinade.
Cover or seal; chill 8 hours, turning occasionally.
3. Follow the grill's instructions
for using wood chunks. Grill
brisket, fat side up, over *Indirect
Low* heat until golden brown,
about 3^1/$_2$ hours, keeping the grill
temperature about 300°F.
4. Brush brisket with 1 cup Texas
Barbecue Sauce; wrap in heavy-
duty aluminum foil. Continue to
grill over *Indirect Low* heat until
very tender, about 1^1/$_2$ hours more.
5. Remove from grill; let rest for
about 15 minutes. Unwrap brisket.
Slice thinly. Serve with remaining
sauce. Yield: 6 to 8 servings.

Barbecued Pork Shoulder

INDIRECT • MEDIUM
Prep: 30 min. • Cook: 7 hrs. • Other: 1 hr.

2 quarts white vinegar
$1/4$ cup ground cayenne pepper, divided
5 oranges, quartered and divided
5 lemons, quartered and divided
$1/2$ cup firmly packed brown sugar
$1/4$ cup ground black pepper
2 tablespoons fresh lemon juice
1 (7- to 8-pound) bone-in pork shoulder roast
1 (2-pound) package hickory chunks, soaked in water for at least 30 minutes

1. Bring vinegar, 2 tablespoons ground cayenne pepper, 3 oranges, and 3 lemons to a boil in a Dutch oven over medium heat; cook 10 minutes. Remove vinegar mixture from heat, and cool.
2. Combine remaining 2 tablespoons ground cayenne pepper, brown sugar, and next 2 ingredients. Rub evenly over pork. Drizzle 1 cup vinegar mixture over pork; set aside 2 cups vinegar mixture for basting, and reserve remaining mixture to fill the water pan.
3. Prepare charcoal fire in smoker; let burn 15 to 20 minutes.
4. Follow the smoker's instructions for using wood chunks. Drain half of wood chunks, and place on coals. Place water pan in smoker; add vinegar mixture and remaining 2 oranges and 2 lemons to depth of fill line. Place pork on lower food rack; cover with smoker lid.
5. Grill the roast over *Indirect Medium* heat 3 hours. Turn and grill an additional 3 to 4 hours (the internal temperature should reach 190°F), basting with reserved 2 cups vinegar mixture every hour and adding more charcoal, remaining half of wood chunks, and vinegar mixture to smoker as needed. Yield: 10 servings.

Pork Chops with Tangy Barbecue Sauce

DIRECT • MEDIUM-HIGH
Prep: 5 min. • Cook: 8 min.

Stir up Tangy Barbecue Sauce ahead so that these chops will be a snap to prepare.

8 (4-ounce) boneless pork loin chops ($1/2$ inch thick)
Tangy Barbecue Sauce (page 83)

1. Grill pork chops over *Direct Medium-High* heat until the meat is barely pink in the center and firm to the touch on the surface, 6 to 8 minutes, turning once and basting with 1 cup Tangy Barbecue Sauce. Serve with additional barbecue sauce. Yield: 8 servings.

Chicken with White Barbecue Sauce

INDIRECT • MEDIUM
Prep: 7 min. • Cook: 50 min. • Other: 8 hrs.

4 chicken legs
White Barbecue Sauce (page 83)

1. Place the chicken in a large zip-top freezer bag; pour $3/4$ cup sauce over chicken, turning to coat. Seal bag, and marinate in the refrigerator 8 hours, turning occasionally. Cover and chill remaining sauce.
2. Remove the chicken from the sauce, discarding sauce in the bag. Grill chicken over *Indirect Medium* heat until the juices run clear and the meat is no longer pink at the bone, 40 to 50 minutes, turning once. Serve with remaining sauce. Yield: 4 servings.

Hickory-Grilled Jerk Chicken

INDIRECT • MEDIUM
Prep: 20 min. • Cook: 10 min. • Other: 8$1/2$ hrs.

Wet Jerk Rub, divided (page 84)
6 (4-ounce) skinned and boned chicken breasts
Hickory chips, soaked in water for at least 30 minutes
4 cups cooked long-grain rice, warm
3 tablespoons fresh lime juice
2 tablespoons peeled, grated ginger
$1/2$ teaspoon freshly grated nutmeg
$1/4$ teaspoon salt

1. Measure $1/2$ cup Wet Jerk Rub, and set aside. Rub the remaining 1 cup paste all over the chicken. Place chicken in a large zip-top freezer bag; seal bag, and marinate in refrigerator 8 hours.
2. Follow the grill's instructions for using wood chips. Grill the chicken over *Direct Medium-High* heat until the meat is firm to the touch and no longer pink in the center, 8 to 10 minutes, turning once. Transfer chicken to a platter, and keep warm.
3. Combine rice and remaining ingredients; toss gently. Spoon rice evenly onto each individual serving plate. Top rice with chicken. Serve immediately. Serve with reserved Wet Jerk Rub. Yield: 6 servings.

Think of chicken as a blank canvas, ready to take on any flavor you can dish up.

sassy sauces 'n' seasonings

Whatever style of barbecue you enjoy, rubs, marinades, and sauces kick up the flavor. When you add just the right sauce to your plate, the experience becomes exceptional.

Sampling sauce is like taking a mini tour of the South. North Carolina is famous for its vinegar-based varieties, while South Carolina's sauce is mustard-tart and sugar-sweet. Texas serves up a thick, sweet sauce with brisket, and farther east in North Alabama, a mayonnaise-based sauce is synonymous with barbecue chicken.

Thin sauces are for basting whole and half hogs during the smoking process. Thicker, more sugary (or mayonnaise-based) sauces are for brushing on at the end of cooking, chopping into the meat, or pouring on a sandwich. The sauces here can all be made ahead and refrigerated for up to one week.

Sweet Mustard Barbecue Sauce

Prep: 8 min. • Cook: 12 min.

Here's a sweeter, slightly thicker version of a traditional South Carolina sauce. Few "red" sauces are allowed in the Carolinas.

1 cup apple cider vinegar
2/3 cup prepared mustard
1/2 cup sugar
2 tablespoons prepared chili powder
1 teaspoon white pepper
1 teaspoon black pepper
1/4 teaspoon ground cayenne pepper
1/2 teaspoon hot sauce
2 tablespoons butter
1/2 teaspoon soy sauce

Sweet Mustard Barbecue Sauce

North Carolina Eastern-Style Barbecue Sauce

Smoky Chipotle 'Cue Sauce

1. Stir together first 8 ingredients in a saucepan over medium heat; bring to a boil, reduce heat, and simmer 10 minutes. Remove from heat, and stir in butter and soy sauce. Serve with barbecued pork or chicken. Yield: about 2 cups.

North Carolina Eastern-Style Barbecue Sauce

Prep: 5 min.

This vinegar-based basting sauce is widely used for North Carolina-style pickin's, where the cavity of the pig is sloshed with sauce so the sauce seeps into the meat during smoking.

7 cups white vinegar
1 cup ginger ale
3 tablespoons plus 1 teaspoon dried crushed red pepper
1 to 2 tablespoons ground black pepper

1. Stir together all ingredients until well blended. Serve over pork barbecue.
Yield: 2 quarts.

Smoky Chipotle 'Cue Sauce

Prep: 5 min. • Cook: 35 min.

You'll never consider store-bought sauce ordinary again once you add these 3 magic ingredients.

2 (18-ounce) bottles barbecue sauce
2 canned chipotle chile peppers
2 tablespoons brown sugar
1 tablespoon chili powder

1. Process all ingredients in a blender until smooth. Pour into a saucepan, and bring to a boil over medium high heat. Reduce heat; simmer 30 minutes. Yield: about 2½ cups.

White Barbecue Sauce

Prep: 5 min.

1½ cups mayonnaise
⅓ cup apple cider vinegar
¼ cup lemon juice
2 tablespoons sugar
2 tablespoons freshly ground black pepper
2 tablespoons white wine Worcestershire sauce

1. Combine all ingredients in a small bowl; stir well. Use to marinate chicken or pork before grilling. After marinating, bring sauce to a boil before using it to baste during cooking. Boil for 1 full minute. Yield: 2¼ cups.

Tangy Barbecue Sauce

Prep: 8 min. • Cook: 34 min.

1 large onion, finely chopped
2 tablespoons butter, melted
2½ cups ketchup
1 cup white vinegar
1 cup water
⅔ cup firmly packed dark brown sugar
¼ cup Worcestershire sauce
2 tablespoons cracked black pepper
2 tablespoons chili sauce
1 tablespoon salt

1. Cook onion in butter in a large saucepan over medium heat until tender, stirring often. Add ketchup and remaining ingredients. Bring to a boil; cover, reduce heat, and simmer 30 minutes.
Yield: 6 cups.

White Barbecue Sauce

Tangy Barbecue Sauce

Vinegar Sauce

Prep: 8 min. • Cook: 17 min.

2 cups apple cider vinegar
1/2 cup white vinegar
1/2 cup apple juice
1/4 cup firmly packed brown sugar
1 tablespoon kosher salt
1/2 tablespoon freshly ground
   black pepper
1/2 teaspoon ground cayenne
   pepper
1/2 teaspoon paprika

1. Place all ingredients in a sauce-pan, and bring to a boil; reduce heat, and simmer 15 minutes. Refrigerate until ready to use. Reheat, if desired. Yield: about 3¼ cups.

Texas Barbecue Sauce

Prep: 10 min. • Cook: 5 min.

2 cups ketchup
1/2 cup white vinegar
1/2 cup honey
1/2 cup water
2 teaspoons dried crushed green
   pepper
1 tablespoon minced onion
2 tablespoons Worcestershire
   sauce
1/4 teaspoon ground black pepper
Dash of garlic powder
Dash of ground cayenne pepper

1. Bring all ingredients to a boil in a large saucepan over medium-high heat, stirring often. Serve with bar-becued beef. Yield: 3½ cups.

Barbecue Rub

Prep: 8 min.

1 cup firmly packed dark brown
   sugar
1/2 cup granulated garlic
1/2 cup kosher salt
1/2 cup paprika
2 tablespoons dried minced onion
1 tablespoon dry mustard
1 tablespoon Creole seasoning
1 tablespoon chili powder
1 tablespoon ground cayenne
   pepper
1 tablespoon ground cumin
1 tablespoon ground black
   pepper

1. Stir together all ingredients in a bowl. Store in an airtight contain-er. Use to rub on chicken or pork before grilling. Yield: about 3 cups.

Chipotle Rub

Prep: 5 min.

The simple flavors in this rub allow the complex heat of chipotle chile peppers to take front and center.

2 to 3 canned chipotle chile
   peppers
1/4 cup firmly packed brown sugar
1 tablespoon chili powder
1 teaspoon salt

1. Chop chile peppers; stir together peppers, brown sugar, chili powder, and salt to form a paste. Rub on ribs before grilling. Yield: 1/3 cup.

Wet Jerk Rub

Prep: 12 min

Using fresh ingredients gives this rub vibrant flavor. Store seldom-used spices, such as coriander seeds, whole allspice, and whole nutmeg, in the freezer in moisture-proof containers. To grind whole spices in a pinch, use the smallest holes on your cheese grater.

4 cups coarsely chopped green
   onions
1/4 cup fresh thyme leaves
3 tablespoons peeled, grated
   ginger
1 tablespoon freshly ground
   pepper
1 tablespoon freshly ground
   coriander seeds
2 tablespoons vegetable oil
2 tablespoons fresh lime juice
2 teaspoons salt
2 teaspoons freshly ground
   allspice
1 teaspoon freshly ground
   nutmeg
1 teaspoon ground cinnamon
5 garlic cloves, peeled and halved
3 bay leaves
1 to 2 habanero peppers, halved
   and seeded

1. Position knife blade in food processor bowl; add all ingredi-ents, and process until smooth, stopping to scrape down sides. Use to rub or brush onto chicken or fish before grilling. Yield: 1½ cups.

here's the rub

If you're not already familiar with the dry rub, it's a classic seasoning blend common on ribs that's also good on briskets, pork chops, chicken, and more. A rub forms something of a crust that seals in the juices during cook-ing. You can also add a small amount of liquid such as olive oil or crushed garlic with its juice to a rub and form a paste. A paste is easy to apply to meat because it clings to the food well. You can apply a rub or paste to food up to 24 hours before cooking for maximum flavor. Or team a sauce with a rub for even more flavor.

Experiment with your favorite spices and herbs to create your own rub. Combine Mexican flavors such as chili powder, granulated onion, and dried oregano to rub onto beef for fajitas. Or blend together minced fresh herbs such as chives, parsley, and rosemary to infuse lamb or chicken with fragrant flavor. Once you start experimenting with herbs and spices, you'll love the possibilities that rubs have to offer.

here's your 'cue

Grilling your way to greatness begins with knowing the basics. Here, in a nutshell, is everything, from choosing wood chips to the best way to baste.

Much of what sets grilled food apart are deep, seared flavors and aromatic wisps of smoke. When food sizzles directly over the hot cooking grate, it develops layers of great tastes and gorgeous grill marks. Juices drip into the grill and turn to smoke that adds an irresistible aroma.

Grilling over direct heat also allows you to caramelize sauces on the surface of the food. If you are using barbecue sauce, be aware that most commercial barbecue sauces contain a lot of sugar or other sweeteners. The sweeter they are the more likely they will just plain burn. Wait until the final 15 minutes of cooking time to brush on a sweet sauce, and it will turn to a delicious, glistening glaze.

Give your food a bolder sense of smokiness by using wood chips or chunks. Soak them in water before adding them to the grill. Some gas grills have "smoker boxes," which sit between the burners and get hot enough for the wood to smolder. For a char-

coal grill, just drop the wood over the hot coals. As always, keep the lid closed to trap the rising smoke. We use wood chips or chunks in combination with indirect heat. The food sits in the middle of the cooking grate and the heat is

off to either side of the food. The moderate, circulating heat cooks large cuts of meat slowly, giving the smoke time to penetrate.

For more advice on grilling like a pro, check out the tips collected above.

10 secrets to grade-A grilling

1. **Go all out.** Buy the best meat you can find. Even the richest sauces can't save a poor piece of meat.

2. **Be organized.** Have food, marinade, sauces, and equipment grillside and ready to go before you start cooking. Allow meats to stand at room temperature 20 to 30 minutes before grilling.

3. **Try woodworking.** Hickory and mesquite give the strongest flavor and are the most common, but don't be afraid to try others, including alder, apple, cherry, grapevine, hickory, maple, and oak. Each has its own characteristics for you to discover.

4. **Gauge your fuel.** Make sure you have enough gas or charcoal before you start.

5. **Go for flavor.** Avoid using lighter fluid because it can cause bitter flavor. For the best taste, start the fire using a chimney starter or paraffin lighter cubes, and allow your charcoal to cook down and turn ashen before grilling your food.

6. **Ban the burn.** Flare-ups lead to burned food, so trim any excess fat and skin from meats to prevent the drips that can cause flare-ups.

7. **Turn, don't stab.** Use tongs or a spatula to turn meat; don't use a carving fork. This way, the meat's flavorful juices won't seep out early.

8. **Keep it covered.** When indirectly grilling, keep the grill covered, and resist the temptation to peek. Each peek loses built-up heat.

9. **Never desert your post.** Even though grilling is easy, it requires vigilance to prevent flare-ups and other potential problems.

10. **Give it a rest.** Meats are juicier and taste better if given the chance to rest for a few minutes after being removed from the flame.

bold new burgers and sandwiches

These burgers and sandwiches feature some feisty new flavors hot off the grill. From creative new toppings to highlighting classic combinations, these sandwiches showcase the best your grill has to offer.

BLT 'n' Tuna Sandwich

DIRECT • HIGH
Prep: 10 min. • Cook: 9 min.

4 (4- to 6-ounce) tuna fillets
  ($^3/_4$ inch thick)
Extra-virgin olive oil
$^1/_2$ teaspoon salt
$^1/_4$ teaspoon freshly ground black
  pepper
8 slices French bread, cut
  diagonally ($^3/_4$ inch thick)
Basil Mayonnaise
Bibb lettuce
8 basil leaves
2 to 3 medium tomatoes, thinly
  sliced
8 slices bacon, cooked

1. Lightly brush or spray tuna fillets with oil; sprinkle with salt and pepper.
2. Grill fillets over *Direct High* heat until opaque in the center, 6 to 8 minutes, turning once.
3. Lightly brush or spray bread slices with oil. Grill over *Direct High* heat until golden, 30 to 60 seconds, turning once.
4. Spread Basil Mayonnaise evenly on 1 side of each bread slice. Layer 4 bread slices with lettuce, basil, tuna, tomato slices, more basil, and bacon; top with remaining bread slices. Yield: 4 sandwiches.

Unlock onion's natural sweetness in this tempting marmalade.

Basil Mayonnaise

Prep: 5 min.

Although the taste of fresh garlic is far superior to bottled minced garlic, bottled will do when you're in a hurry. Keep it refrigerated once opened.

$^1/_2$ cup mayonnaise
2 tablespoons finely chopped
  fresh basil
$^1/_4$ teaspoon minced fresh garlic
$^1/_4$ teaspoon freshly ground black
  pepper

1. Mix all ingredients in a bowl. Yield: $^1/_2$ cup.

Peppered Flank Steak Sandwich with Onion Marmalade

DIRECT • MEDIUM
Prep: 25 min. • Cook: 47 min.

Besides adding a depth of flavor, pepper cuts the slight sweetness of the onion marmalade. This steak can be served with or without the bun.

$^1/_3$ cup granulated sugar
1 teaspoon vegetable oil
3 cups finely chopped yellow onion
$^1/_2$ teaspoon salt, divided
$^1/_4$ cup fresh orange juice
1 tablespoon bourbon (optional)
2 teaspoons Dijon mustard
5 garlic cloves, crushed
1 (1$^1/_2$-pound) flank steak
1 to 2 tablespoons coarsely
  ground black pepper
6 whole wheat hamburger buns,
  split and toasted

Don't be afraid to augment your favorite condiments. A pinch of herbs or a squeeze of citrus brings out new and interesting flavors.

1. Cook sugar in oil in a large skillet over medium heat, stirring constantly, about 10 minutes or until golden.
2. Add chopped onion and $^1/_4$ teaspoon salt (mixture will lump), and cook 20 minutes or until golden, stirring often.
3. Stir in orange juice and, if desired, bourbon; cook 5 minutes or until liquid evaporates. Set aside and keep warm.
4. Combine Dijon mustard, the remaining $^1/_4$ teaspoon salt, and garlic; spread mixture over both sides of steak. Sprinkle steak with pepper, and press gently into mustard mixture.
5. Grill steak over *Direct Medium* heat, 10 to 12 minutes, turning once. Cut steak diagonally across the grain into thin slices.
6. Spoon steak onto bottom halves of buns; top evenly with onion mixture, and cover with bun tops. Yield: 6 servings.

Peppered Flank Steak Sandwich with Onion Marmalade

Jalapeño Cheeseburger

Open-Faced Southwestern
Chicken Sandwich

Jalapeño Cheeseburgers

DIRECT • MEDIUM-HIGH

Prep: 15 min. • Cook: 15 min. • Other: 30 min.

2 pounds ground chuck
2 tablespoons grated yellow onion
1 1/2 teaspoons Greek seasoning
1 teaspoon salt
1 teaspoon black pepper
1 (3-ounce) package cream
   cheese, softened
2 tablespoons minced pickled
   jalapeño pepper
4 hamburger buns
Toppings: lettuce leaves, onion
   slices, tomato slices

1. Combine first 5 ingredients; shape into 8 thin patties.
2. Stir together cream cheese and jalapeño pepper; spoon evenly in center of 4 patties. (Do not spread to edges.) Top with remaining patties, pressing edges to seal. Cover and chill 30 minutes.
3. Grill the patties over *Direct Medium-High* heat until medium, 12 to 15 minutes, turning once. Serve patties on buns with desired toppings. Yield: 4 servings.

Open-Faced Southwestern Chicken Sandwiches

DIRECT • MEDIUM

Prep: 15 min. • Cook: 20 min.

4 skinned and boned chicken
   breasts
2 tablespoons finely chopped
   fresh cilantro
2 tablespoons vegetable oil
1 garlic clove, minced
2 teaspoons prepared chili powder
1/4 teaspoon ground cayenne pepper
4 sourdough bread slices (1 inch
   thick)
1 cup (4 ounces) shredded
   Mexican cheese blend
1/3 cup mayonnaise
Orange-Black Bean Salsa

1. Place chicken between 2 sheets of heavy-duty plastic wrap, and flatten to 1/2-inch thickness using a meat mallet or rolling pin.
2. Stir together cilantro and next 4 ingredients. Spread on chicken.

Grill the chicken over *Direct Medium* heat until firm and the juices run clear, 8 to 12 minutes, turning once.
3. Toast bread over *Direct Medium* heat 1 to 2 minutes, turning once. Stir together cheese and mayonnaise. Spread on toasted bread slices. Place bread, cheese mixture side up, on a baking sheet.
4. Grill on baking sheet over *Direct Medium* heat until cheese melts, 4 to 6 minutes. Place chicken on bread; serve with Orange-Black Bean Salsa. Yield: 4 servings.

Orange-Black Bean Salsa

Prep: 15 min. • Other: 1 hr.

1 navel orange
1 plum tomato
1/2 medium cucumber
1 avocado
1/3 cup finely chopped red onion
1/2 (15-ounce) can black beans,
   rinsed and drained
1 1/2 tablespoons finely chopped
   fresh cilantro
1 tablespoon olive oil
1 1/2 tablespoons fresh lime juice
2 teaspoons red wine vinegar
1/8 teaspoon dried crushed red
   pepper
1/8 teaspoon salt

1. Peel, section, and finely dice orange. Finely dice tomato. Peel, seed, and finely dice cucumber and avocado.
2. Combine finely diced ingredients with onion, beans, and cilantro in a bowl. Whisk together oil and next 4 ingredients. Toss with orange mixture. Cover and chill for 1 to 2 hours. Yield: about 2 cups.

> To make your own cheese blend, mix strong-flavored cheeses with mild varieties.

best burger tips

• For moist, juicy burgers, avoid selecting finely ground beef. Look for a coarse grind.
• Skip the mess of mixing ground beef by hand by combining ingredients in a zip-top freezer bag. Squeeze the bag just until mixture is blended.
• Wet hands while forming burgers in order to keep meat from sticking to your fingers.
• Ground beef can be frozen up to 3 months. Store in the refrigerator up to 2 days before use.

Open-Faced Summer Sandwiches

DIRECT • MEDIUM

Prep: 10 min. • Cook: 14 min.

2 large tomatoes, cut crosswise
   into 1/2-inch slices
1 teaspoon salt
1/2 teaspoon black pepper
2 large yellow onions, cut
   crosswise into 1/2-inch slices
1/4 cup olive oil, divided
4 French bread slices (1 inch thick)
1/2 cup mayonnaise
3 tablespoons pesto
1 cup thinly sliced ripe olives
2 1/2 tablespoons finely chopped
   fresh mint (optional)

1. Sprinkle tomato slices evenly with salt and pepper; set aside.
2. Lightly brush both sides of onion slices with oil. Grill onions over *Direct Medium* heat until tender and browned, 10 to 12 minutes, turning once.
3. Lightly brush both sides of bread slices with oil. Grill the slices over *Direct Medium* heat until lightly browned, 1 to 2 minutes, turning once.
4. Stir together mayonnaise and pesto; spread evenly on 1 side of each bread slice. Top evenly with tomato and onion slices; sprinkle with olives. Sprinkle with mint, if desired. Yield: 4 servings.

pizza on the grill

Grilling makes delicious pizzas. New tastes and textures come from first grilling one side of the crusts, then turning and topping the crust and grilling it until the tasty rounds are crisp.

When you think of your grill as a summer oven, cooking outdoors goes far beyond burgers and steaks. Individual pizzas are easy to grill and ideal for casual summer entertaining. Begin with our basic Pizza Crusts (below); then choose from a selection of toppings.

Pizza Crusts

DIRECT • MEDIUM
Prep: 5 min. • Cook: 3 min.

1 (32-ounce) package frozen
    bread dough
Olive oil

1. Thaw bread dough. Cut dough into 4 balls. On a lightly floured surface, roll each ball flat into a round about ¼ inch thick, leaving the dough a little thicker at the edge than in the middle.
2. Lightly brush one side of each round with oil, and place oiled side down on the cooking grate. Grill the bread over *Direct Medium* heat until light grill marks appear on bottoms, 2 to 3 minutes. Move crust to a work surface, with the grilled sides facing up. Arrange toppings and finish grilling as described in any of the following recipes. Yield: 4 pizza crusts.

Grilled Pepper Pizzas

DIRECT • MEDIUM
Prep: 8 min. • Cook: 15 min.

Pizza Crusts (recipe at left)
1 medium green bell pepper
1 medium yellow bell pepper
1 medium red bell pepper
1 cup tomato sauce
2 garlic cloves, minced
1 teaspoon salt
2 cups (8 ounces) shredded
    mozzarella cheese

1. Grill first side of pizza crusts as described in recipe at left.
2. Cut peppers in half through stem; remove seeds.
3. Grill the peppers over *Direct Medium* heat until charred and blistered, about 8 to 10 minutes, turning occasionally. Cool to touch; peel and cut into thin strips.
4. Combine tomato sauce, garlic, and salt; spread evenly over grilled side of pizza crusts. Sprinkle with cheese, and top with pepper strips.
5. Grill crusts over *Direct Medium* heat until slightly crisp, about 3 to 5 minutes. Yield: 4 pizzas.

Bacon-Cheese Pizzas

DIRECT • MEDIUM
Prep: 5 min. • Cook: 5 min.

Pizza Crusts (recipe at left)
1 cup pizza sauce
1 (8-ounce) package shredded
    three-cheese blend
12 bacon slices, cooked and
    crumbled

1. Grill first side of pizza crusts as described in recipe at left.
2. Spread grilled side of pizza crusts evenly with pizza sauce; sprinkle with cheese and bacon.
3. Grill crusts over *Direct Medium* heat until slightly crisp, about 3 to 5 minutes. Yield: 4 pizzas.

Pesto Ham 'n' Potato Pizzas

DIRECT • MEDIUM
Prep: 15 min. • Cook: 25 min.

1 pound small red potatoes
½ cup bottled pesto
Pizza Crusts (recipe at left)
1 teaspoon salt
½ teaspoon black pepper
8 ounces thinly sliced ham
2 cups (8 ounces) grated Gruyère
    or Swiss cheese
¼ cup thinly sliced green
    onions

1. Bring potatoes and water to cover them to a boil in a large saucepan over medium-high heat; cover, reduce heat, and simmer 15 to 20 minutes or until tender. Drain and cool slightly. Cut potatoes into thin slices; toss with ¼ cup pesto.
2. Grill first side of pizza crusts as described in recipe at left.
3. Spread grilled side of each pizza crust with 1 tablespoon pesto.
4. Top each pizza crust evenly with potatoes; sprinkle with salt and pepper. Top with ham and remaining ingredients.
5. Grill crusts over *Direct Medium* heat until slightly crisp, about 3 to 5 minutes. Yield: 4 pizzas.

Grilled Tomato Pizzas

Grilled Tomato Pizzas

DIRECT • MEDIUM
Prep: 10 min. • Cook: 5 min.

Pizza Crusts (recipe on opposite
   page)
1 cup crumbled feta cheese
¹/₂ cup finely chopped fresh basil
2 teaspoons minced garlic
1 teaspoon salt
¹/₂ teaspoon black pepper
3 large red tomatoes, cut
   crosswise into ¹/₄-inch slices
3 large yellow tomatoes, cut
   crosswise into ¹/₄-inch slices
Extra-virgin olive oil

1. Grill first side of pizza crusts as
described in Pizza Crusts recipe.
2. Combine the feta cheese and
the next 4 ingredients.
3. Lightly brush tomato slices on
both sides with oil; grill over *Direct
Medium* heat just until warm,
about 2 minutes, without turning.
4. Arrange tomato slices evenly on
grilled side of pizza crusts; sprinkle
evenly with cheese mixture.
5. Grill crusts over *Direct Medium*
heat until slightly crisp, about 3 to
5 minutes. Yield: 4 pizzas.

Sausage-Spinach Pizzas

DIRECT • MEDIUM
Prep: 10 min. • Cook: 15 min.

To give this pizza extra heat, use
Monterey Jack cheese with peppers.

Pizza Crusts (recipe on opposite
   page)
1 (10-ounce) package frozen
   chopped spinach, thawed
¹/₂ pound ground hot pork
   sausage
2 cups (8 ounces) shredded
   Monterey Jack cheese
1 teaspoon salt
¹/₂ teaspoon black pepper

1. Grill first side of pizza crusts as
described in Pizza Crusts recipe.
2. Drain spinach well, pressing
between layers of paper towels.
3. Cook sausage in a large skillet,
stirring until it crumbles and is no
longer pink; drain well.
4. Combine spinach, sausage,
cheese, salt, and pepper; spoon
over grilled side of pizza crusts.
5. Grill crusts over *Direct Medium*
heat until slightly crisp, about 3 to
5 minutes. Yield: 4 pizzas.

Southwestern Pizzas

DIRECT • MEDIUM
Prep: 10 min. • Cook: 5 min.

Pizza Crusts (recipe on opposite
   page)
2 cups diced cooked chicken
1 cup canned black beans, rinsed
   and drained
¹/₂ cup finely chopped fresh cilantro
2 garlic cloves, minced
1 teaspoon ground cumin
1 teaspoon dried crushed red
   pepper
1 teaspoon salt
1 cup chunky salsa
1 (8-ounce) package shredded
   Monterey Jack cheese with
   peppers

1. Grill first side of pizza crusts as
described in Pizza Crusts recipe.
2. Combine chicken and next 6
ingredients in a large bowl.
3. Spread grilled side of pizza crusts
with salsa; sprinkle with half of
cheese. Top with chicken mixture;
sprinkle with remaining cheese.
4. Grill crusts over *Direct Medium*
heat until slightly crisp, about
3 to 5 minutes. Yield: 4 pizzas.

salsa fiesta

Salsas take to grilling like kids to cookies. Scoop up these spicy blends with chips while the beef, chicken, or fish sizzles on the grill. Save some salsa to crown the entrée, too.

Grilled Corn Salsa

DIRECT • MEDIUM
Prep: 10 min. • Cook: 10 min.

Fresh corn has a natural sweetness that makes a great foil to salsa's heat. For best flavor, look for ears of corn with bright green, snug husks and golden brown silks.

6 ears fresh corn, husks and silks removed
1 large red bell pepper, quartered, seeds and stem discarded
3 teaspoons extra-virgin olive oil, divided
$^1/_2$ cup finely diced red onion
$^1/_4$ cup finely diced green chile pepper
1 tablespoon fresh lime juice
$^1/_4$ teaspoon salt

the art of searing

Salsa is a staple on the party circuit for a reason—it's the easiest, tastiest, most versatile appetizer available. But don't limit this finely balanced combination of crunchy, spicy, and tangy to tame tortilla chips. New ways to serve salsa include over baguette slices; spooned over grilled beef, poultry, or fish; as a soup topper; as a side dish; or as a garnish.

Store fresh salsas tightly covered in the refrigerator for up to 5 days. Unopened bottled salsas can be stored at room temperature for up to 6 months. Once opened, refrigerate bottled salsas up to 1 month.

1. Lightly brush corn and bell pepper with 2 teaspoons oil.
2. Grill corn and bell pepper over *Direct Medium* heat about 10 minutes, turning occasionally. Remove from grill; cool. Peel and discard the bell pepper's charred skin.
3. Cut corn from cob, and mince bell pepper.
4. Combine corn, bell pepper, remaining 1 teaspoon oil, onion, and remaining ingredients; serve at room temperature. Yield: $3^1/_2$ cups.

Tomatillo Salsa

Prep: 20 min. • Cook: 15 min.

Tomatillos have a tangy flavor and look like green cherry tomatoes in papery husks.

$2^1/_2$ pounds fresh tomatillos
6 garlic cloves, unpeeled
4 large fresh jalapeño peppers
2 large onions, quartered
$2^1/_2$ tablespoons vegetable oil
$^1/_2$ to $^3/_4$ teaspoon salt
$^1/_2$ teaspoon freshly ground pepper
$^1/_2$ cup chopped fresh cilantro
$^1/_2$ cup whipping cream

1. Remove and discard tomatillo husks; rinse tomatillos. Toss tomatillos and next 3 ingredients in vegetable oil; spread vegetables in a 13- x 9-inch pan.
2. Bake at 500°F for 15 minutes or just until vegetables are charred; cool completely. Remove and discard stems (but not seeds) from jalapeño peppers. Peel garlic, discarding skins. Drain tomatillos, discarding any liquid.

3. Pulse roasted vegetables in a food processor 4 times or until coarsely chopped. Transfer mixture to a bowl; stir in salt and remaining ingredients. Yield: 4 cups.

Grilled Serrano Salsa

DIRECT • MEDIUM
Prep: 10 min. • Cook: 10 min. • Other: 1 hr.

The heat offered by serrano chiles makes them classic salsa add-ins.

6 serrano chile peppers
1 pound plum tomatoes, finely diced
2 tablespoons finely diced red onion
$^1/_4$ cup fresh orange juice
2 tablespoons finely diced yellow bell pepper
2 tablespoons finely chopped fresh cilantro
1 tablespoon rice vinegar
$^1/_2$ teaspoon salt
$^1/_2$ teaspoon granulated sugar
Garnishes: fresh cilantro sprigs, red onion wedge

1. Grill peppers over *Direct Medium* heat until evenly charred on all sides, 8 to 10 minutes, turning every 3 or 4 minutes. Cool. Peel peppers, if desired, and finely chop.
2. Combine serrano peppers, tomatoes, and next 7 ingredients; cover and chill at least 1 hour. Garnish, if desired. Yield: 2 cups.

Note: For hotter salsa, use 7 or 8 serrano peppers. For milder salsa, use 2 or 3 serrano peppers.

Three-Tomato Salsa

Prep: 25 min. • Other: 3 hrs.

1 cup chopped red tomato
1 cup chopped yellow tomato
1 cup chopped green tomato
1/2 cup diced red onion
2 garllc cloves, minced
1/3 cup olive oil
1/4 cup red wine vinegar
2 tablespoons chopped fresh
  cilantro
1 tablespoon chopped fresh
  parsley
1 tablespoon chopped fresh
  chives
1/8 teaspoon salt
1/8 teaspoon ground cayenne
  pepper
1/8 teaspoon ground black pepper

1. Combine all ingredients; cover and chill 3 to 4 hours. Yield: 3 cups.

Black Bean-Corn Salsa

Prep: 15 min. • Cook: 7 min.

3 ears white corn
3/4 cup water
3 medium tomatoes
2 jalapeño peppers
2 (15-ounce) cans black beans,
  rinsed and drained
1 cup chopped fresh cilantro
1/3 cup fresh lime juice
1/4 teaspoon salt
1/4 teaspoon freshly ground
  pepper
2 avocados
Tortilla chips

1. Cut corn from cobs into a saucepan; add ¾ cup water, and bring to a boil. Cover, reduce heat, and simmer 6 to 7 minutes or until tender. Drain corn; transfer to a large bowl.

2. Peel, seed, and dice tomatoes; add to corn. Seed and mince jalapeño peppers; add to corn mixture with beans and next 4 ingredients, stirring gently. Chill up to 24 hours.

3. Before serving, peel and dice avocados; stir into corn mixture, and serve with tortilla chips. Yield: 8 cups.

salsa for supper

Black beans add protein to the simple salsa at left. Turn it into a filling taco salad by pouring it over tortilla chips and topping it with shredded lettuce and your favorite shredded Mexican cheese blend.

Grilled Serrano Salsa

versatile veggies

This collection of 15 of our all-time favorite veggie sides makes it easy to find just what you need to round out your grilled menus. It includes high-flavor surprises you can grill alongside the entrée as well as quick kitchen medleys to make ahead or in a jiffy while the grill's glowing.

Grilled Asparagus Salad with Orange Vinaigrette

DIRECT • MEDIUM
Prep: 15 min. • Cook: 8 min. • Other: 1 hr.

This easy-to-prepare salad is as impressive as it is flavorful. Grill the asparagus spears ahead of time to make assembly a breeze.

1 pound fresh asparagus
1 tablespoon grated orange zest
$^1/_4$ cup fresh orange juice
$^1/_3$ cup olive oil
$^1/_4$ cup balsamic vinegar
1 teaspoon Dijon mustard
$^1/_2$ teaspoon salt
$^1/_4$ teaspoon black pepper
1 pound mixed gourmet salad greens
4 cooked bacon slices, crumbled (optional)
Orange zest strips

1. Snap off tough ends of asparagus and discard; place asparagus spears in a shallow dish.
2. Combine orange zest and next 6 ingredients in a jar; cover tightly. Shake jar vigorously. Pour one-third of vinaigrette over asparagus spears; cover and chill 1 hour. Drain.
3. Grill asparagus spears over *Direct Medium* heat until crisp-tender, 6 to 8 minutes, turning occasionally; cool.
4. Toss together salad greens, remaining vinaigrette, and, if desired, crumbled bacon; mound salad onto 4 plates. Loosely tie asparagus into 4 bundles with orange zest strips. Yield: 4 servings.

Easy Vegetable Kabobs

DIRECT • MEDIUM
Prep: 15 min. • Cook: 25 min.

Soak wooden skewers in water for 30 minutes before adding the vegetables.

8 small mushroom caps
2 small zucchini, cut crosswise into 8 slices
1 medium yellow bell pepper, cut into $^3/_4$-inch pieces
1 small red onion, quartered and separated into leaves
$^1/_2$ cup unsalted butter, melted
1 tablespoon finely chopped fresh basil
1 teaspoon garlic powder

1. Thread vegetables evenly onto 12-inch skewers.
2. Stir together melted butter, basil, and garlic powder; reserve $^1/_4$ cup butter mixture; set aside.
3. Grill the vegetables over *Direct Medium* heat until tender, 20 to 25 minutes, turning and basting with remaining butter mixture every 5 minutes. Serve with reserved butter mixture. Yield: 4 servings.

Grilled Stuffed Onions

DIRECT • MEDIUM-HIGH
Prep: 15 min. • Cook: 25 min.

$1^1/_2$ cups herb-seasoned stuffing mix
1 cup (4 ounces) shredded sharp Cheddar cheese
1 teaspoon poultry seasoning
$^1/_3$ cup unsalted butter, melted
$^1/_3$ cup hot water
6 medium yellow onions
Olive oil

1. Stir together first 5 ingredients.
2. Cut each onion crosswise into 3 slices. Spread 2 tablespoons stuffing mixture between slices, and reassemble onions. Place each onion on a 12-inch square piece of heavy-duty aluminum foil lightly brushed with oil; bring opposite corners together, and twist to seal.
3. Grill onions over *Direct Medium-High* heat until tender, about 25 minutes. Yield: 6 servings.

Barbecue Coleslaw

Prep: 15 min.

For even quicker prep time, look for bagged, pre-shredded red and green cabbage in the grocery store. Many stores carry pre-shredded carrot and chopped bell peppers as well.

2 cups shredded red cabbage
2 cups shredded green cabbage
$^1/_2$ cup thinly sliced onion, separated into rings
$^1/_2$ cup shredded carrot
$^1/_4$ cup chopped green or red bell pepper
$^1/_4$ cup coleslaw dressing
$^1/_4$ cup barbecue sauce
$^1/_8$ teaspoon hot sauce

1. Combine first 5 ingredients in a large bowl, tossing gently.
2. Stir together dressing, barbecue sauce, and hot sauce; pour over cabbage mixture, tossing gently. Yield: 8 servings.

Grilled Asparagus Salad
with Orange Vinaigrette

Grilled Vegetables with Cilantro Butter

DIRECT • MEDIUM

Prep: 15 min. • Cook: 30 min. • Other: 30 min.

4 ears fresh corn, unshucked
Cilantro Butter
4 medium tomatoes, halved
4 medium zucchini, cut
   lengthwise into $1/2$-inch slices
$1/2$ teaspoon salt
$1/2$ teaspoon freshly ground black
   pepper
Garnish: fresh cilantro sprigs

1. Soak corn in cold water at least 30 minutes. If necessary, use a weight to keep the corn submerged. Peel back corn husks, leaving them attached at the base of the corn. Remove silks.
2. Spread Cilantro Butter evenly over corn, tomatoes, and zucchini; sprinkle with salt and pepper. Pull husks over corn and use string or a thin strip of husk to tie them at the top.
3. Grill corn over *Direct Medium* heat until tender, about 15 to 20 minutes, turning occasionally. Husk edges will blacken. Meanwhile, grill tomatoes and zucchini over *Direct Medium* heat until well-marked, 8 to 10 minutes, turning once. Remove husks from corn. Serve all vegetables immediately. Garnish, if desired. Yield: 4 servings.

Cilantro Butter

Prep: 7 min.

$1/2$ cup unsalted butter, softened
$1/4$ cup finely chopped fresh cilantro
4 garlic cloves, minced

1. Stir together all ingredients. Store in refrigerator. Soften before using. Yield: $1/2$ cup.

Grilled Summer Squash Salad with Citrus Splash Dressing

DIRECT • MEDIUM

Prep: 15 min. • Cook: 10 min. • Other: 1 hr.

2 tablespoons grated orange
   zest
$3/4$ cup fresh orange juice (about
   3 oranges)
$1/2$ cup fresh lime juice (about
   3 limes)
3 tablespoons honey
2 teaspoons olive oil
$1/2$ teaspoon salt
$1/4$ teaspoon dried crushed red
   pepper
2 medium red onions
4 medium zucchini, each halved
   lengthwise (about $1 1/4$ pounds)
4 medium yellow squash, each
   halved lengthwise (about
   1 pound)
3 tablespoons thinly sliced fresh
   basil

1. Combine first 7 ingredients in a large zip-top freezer bag. Peel onions, leaving root intact; cut each onion into 4 wedges. Add onion, zucchini, and yellow squash to bag. Seal and marinate at room temperature for 1 hour, turning bag occasionally.
2. Drain vegetables in a colander over a bowl, reserving marinade. Grill the vegetables over *Direct Medium* heat until tender, 8 to 10 minutes, turning and basting occasionally with $3/4$ cup of the marinade. Place the vegetables on a serving platter; sprinkle with the basil. Serve vegetables with the remaining marinade. Yield: 4 servings.

> Use this dressing year-round on your favorite combination of vegetables or fruits.

Grilled Corn with Jalapeño-Lime Butter

DIRECT • MEDIUM

Prep: 15 min. • Cook: 15 min. • Other: 1 hr.

$1/2$ cup unsalted butter, softened
2 jalapeño peppers, seeded and
   minced
2 tablespoons grated lime zest
1 teaspoon fresh lime juice
6 ears fresh corn, husks removed
1 tablespoon extra-virgin olive oil
2 teaspoons kosher salt
1 teaspoon freshly ground black
   pepper

1. Combine first 4 ingredients, and shape into a 6-inch log; wrap in wax paper, and chill 1 hour.
2. Lightly brush the corn with oil; sprinkle evenly with salt and pepper.
3. Grill corn over *Direct Medium* heat until tender and golden, 10 to 15 minutes, turning occasionally. Serve with flavored butter. Yield: 6 servings.

Grilled Vegetables with Cilantro Butter

Grilled Fennel and
Radicchio Salad

Grilled Fennel and Radicchio Salad

DIRECT • MEDIUM-HIGH
Prep: 15 min. • Cook: 14 min. • Other: 15 min.

Don't core the fennel when making this recipe. The core holds the slices together so they won't fall through the cooking grate.

4 medium fennel bulbs
1/2 cup fresh orange juice
1/4 cup orange marmalade
2 tablespoons olive oil
1 tablespoon white wine vinegar
2 garlic cloves, minced
1/2 teaspoon salt
1/4 teaspoon freshly ground black pepper
1 small head radicchio, leaves torn into small pieces
Garnish: fennel sprigs

1. Cut fennel bulbs vertically into 1/4-inch slices.
2. Whisk together orange juice and next 6 ingredients until blended. Chill 1/4 cup vinaigrette; pour

remaining vinaigrette over fennel and radicchio separately, tossing gently to coat. Let stand 15 minutes; drain.
3. Grill fennel over *Direct Medium-High* heat until crisp-tender, 10 to 12 minutes, turning once. Grill radicchio over *Direct Medium-High* heat until crisp-tender, about 2 minutes. Toss fennel and radicchio together with chilled vinaigrette; garnish, if desired, and serve immediately. Yield: 5 servings.

Radicchio's bitter bite mellows when paired with the light licorice flavor of fennel.

Bulgur Pilaf

Prep: 15 min. • Cook: 20 min.

Toast pine nuts for this dish in a single layer in a roasting pan. After about 5 minutes at 350°F, you should be able to tell they're done by their aroma.

1 cup chopped onion
1 cup coarsely shredded carrot
2 tablespoons olive oil
1 1/2 cups plus 2 tablespoons bulgur wheat, uncooked
1/2 cup currants
1 teaspoon salt
2 cups water
2 tablespoons pine nuts, toasted

1. Sauté onion and carrot in hot oil in a medium saucepan 5 minutes or until tender. Stir in bulgur, currants, and salt; add water, and bring to a boil. Cover, reduce heat, and simmer 10 minutes or until bulgur is tender and liquid is absorbed. Spoon into serving bowls, and sprinkle with pine nuts. Yield: 5 servings.

Grilled Peppers
and Veggies

Grilled Peppers and Veggies

DIRECT • MEDIUM

Prep: 15 min. • Cook: 12 min. • Other: 2 hrs.

$^3/_4$ cup olive oil

$^1/_4$ cup red wine vinegar

1 tablespoon minced garlic

1 tablespoon finely chopped fresh
rosemary

1 tablespoon finely chopped
fresh basil

1 teaspoon fresh thyme leaves

1 teaspoon salt

$^1/_2$ teaspoon freshly ground black
pepper

1 medium yellow bell pepper

1 medium red bell pepper

1 medium green bell pepper

3 medium zucchini

2 large yellow onions

1 medium eggplant

1. Combine first 8 ingredients in
a large bowl.

2. Cut bell peppers into large
pieces, discarding seeds and
membranes. Cut zucchini in half
crosswise; then cut each piece
in half lengthwise. Cut onions
crosswise into $^1/_3$-inch slices. Slice
eggplant crosswise into $^1/_2$-inch slices.
Add vegetables to marinade; toss to
coat. Marinate at room temperature
for 2 hours.

3. Remove vegetables from marinade, reserving marinade. Grill
over *Direct Medium* heat until tender and charred, about 10 to 12
minutes, basting occasionally with
reserved marinade. Serve vegetables warm, at room temperature,
or cover and chill up to 24 hours.
Yield: 6 to 8 servings.

These foil-wrapped
potatoes look
ordinary, but an
herby surprise
awaits inside.

Thyme for Potatoes

INDIRECT • HIGH

Prep: 15 min. • Cook: 1 hr.

4 small baking potatoes

$1^1/_2$ tablespoons olive oil

1 teaspoon dried thyme

1 teaspoon kosher salt

$^1/_2$ teaspoon dried basil

$^1/_4$ teaspoon freshly ground black
pepper

$^1/_2$ cup minced yellow onion

1 tablespoon minced garlic

1. Cut 1 potato lengthwise into
quarters; place on a 12-inch square
piece of foil. Lightly brush cut
sides with oil. Sprinkle evenly with
one-fourth each of thyme, salt,
basil, and pepper. Top each evenly
with one-fourth each of onion and
garlic. Reassemble potato; tightly
wrap potato in foil. Repeat procedure with remaining potatoes and
ingredients.

2. Grill the potatoes over *Indirect
High* heat until tender, about 1
hour, turning every 15 minutes.
Yield: 4 servings.

Spicy Bean Salad

Prep: 10 min. • Other: 2 hrs.

1 (15-ounce) can great Northern
   beans, rinsed and drained
1 (15-ounce) can black beans,
   rinsed and drained
4 plum tomatoes, chopped
1 medium green bell pepper,
   chopped
3/4 cup chopped green onions
1/2 cup salsa
1/4 cup red wine vinegar
2 tablespoons chopped fresh
   cilantro
1/2 teaspoon salt
1/2 teaspoon pepper

1. Combine all ingredients; cover and refrigerate at least 2 hours. Yield: 6 servings.

Wild Rice with Mushrooms

Prep: 8 min. • Cook: 1 hr., 10 min.

1/4 cup unsalted butter, cut
   into pieces
1 (6-ounce) package wild rice
1 (8-ounce) package sliced fresh
   mushrooms
3 green onions, chopped
1/2 teaspoon salt
1 (14-ounce) can chicken broth
2 tablespoons sherry (optional)
1/2 cup sliced almonds, toasted
   (optional)

1. Melt butter in a 2-quart saucepan over medium heat. Stir in rice, and cook, stirring occasionally, 5 minutes.
2. Add mushrooms and next 4 ingredients to rice mixture; bring to a boil. Cover, reduce heat, and simmer 1 hour and 5 minutes or until rice is done; drain excess liquid, if desired. Fluff rice with a fork; sprinkle with almonds, if desired. Yield: 8 servings.

Note: This recipe can be made ahead in a slow cooker. Combine first 7 ingredients in a 4-quart electric slow cooker; cover and cook on HIGH setting 3 hours. Drain excess liquid, if necessary. Fluff rice with a fork; sprinkle with almonds, if desired.

Grilled Romaine Salad with Buttermilk-Chive Dressing

DIRECT • MEDIUM

Prep: 10 min. • Cook: 17 min.

4 romaine lettuce hearts
1 large red onion
1 to 2 tablespoons olive oil
Buttermilk-Chive Dressing
Kosher salt to taste
Freshly ground black pepper to
   taste
1/2 cup freshly shaved or
   shredded Parmesan cheese

1. Cut romaine hearts in half lengthwise, keeping leaves intact. Cut red onion crosswise into 1/2-inch slices, keeping rings intact; lightly brush with oil, and set aside.
2. Grill the onion slices over *Direct Medium* heat until slices are tender, 10 to 12 minutes, turning once. Set aside.
3. Grill the romaine halves, cut side down, for 3 to 5 minutes or until just wilted. If desired, rotate halves once for cross-hatch marks. Brush warm romaine halves with enough Buttermilk-Chive Dressing to coat them lightly.
4. Place 2 romaine halves on each of 4 salad plates. Sprinkle with salt and pepper to taste. Top each evenly with onion slices and Parmesan cheese. Serve immediately with remaining Buttermilk-Chive Dressing. Yield: 4 servings.

Buttermilk-Chive Dressing

Prep: 10 min.

3/4 cup buttermilk
1/2 cup mayonnaise
2 tablespoons finely chopped
   fresh chives
1 tablespoon minced green onion
1 garlic clove, minced
1/2 teaspoon salt
1/4 teaspoon freshly ground
   black pepper

1. Whisk together all ingredients. Cover; chill until ready to use. Yield: 1 1/4 cups.

Vegetables are a chef's paintbox. They offer an array of colors, textures, and tastes that provide a base for a meal or its crowning glory. Let your eyes (and your taste buds) guide you.

Green Bean, Walnut, and Feta Salad

Prep: 12 min. • Cook: 25 min. • Other: 1 hr.

The intense, earthy flavor of toasted nuts complements the crisp greens.

1 cup coarsely chopped walnuts
3/4 cup olive oil
1/4 cup white wine vinegar
1 tablespoon chopped fresh dill
1/2 teaspoon minced garlic
1/4 teaspoon salt
1/4 teaspoon pepper
1 1/2 pounds fresh green beans
1 small red onion, thinly sliced
1 (4-ounce) package crumbled
   feta cheese

1. Bake walnuts in a shallow pan at 350°F, stirring occasionally, 5 to 10 minutes or until toasted; set aside.
2. Combine oil and next 5 ingredients; cover and chill.
3. Cut beans into thirds, and arrange in a steamer basket over boiling water. Cover and steam 15 minutes or until beans are crisptender. Immediately plunge green beans into cold water to stop cooking process; drain and pat dry.
4. Combine walnuts, beans, onion, and cheese in a large bowl; toss well. Cover and chill. Pour oil mixture over bean mixture 1 hour before serving; toss just before serving. Yield: 6 servings.

bread basket bounty

We offer a trio of options for grilling bread on the side as well as three family faves that just need a short stint in the oven.

Greek Bread

DIRECT • MEDIUM
Prep: 10 min. • Cook: 10 min.

1/3 cup unsalted butter, softened
2 tablespoons mayonnaise
1 (2¹/₂-ounce) jar sliced
   mushrooms, drained
1 (2¹/₄-ounce) can sliced ripe
   olives, drained
2 green onions, chopped
1 (16-ounce) French bread loaf
1 cup (4 ounces) shredded
   mozzarella cheese

1. Stir first 5 ingredients in a medium bowl.
2. Cut bread loaf in half lengthwise. Spread cut side of bottom half evenly with butter mixture; sprinkle with cheese. Cover with bread top. Wrap in heavy-duty aluminum foil.
3. Grill the bread over *Direct Medium* heat until toasted, 8 to 10 minutes, turning once. Yield: 1 loaf.

Texas Toast

DIRECT • MEDIUM
Prep: 5 min. • Cook: 2 min.

2 tablespoons unsalted butter,
   softened
1 garlic clove, minced
8 slices sourdough bread
   (³/₄ inch thick)

1. Combine butter and garlic; spread over 1 side of each bread slice.
2. Grill the bread slices over *Direct Medium* heat until lightly browned, 1 to 2 minutes, turning occasionally. Yield: 8 servings.

Grilled Cheese Bread

DIRECT • MEDIUM
Prep: 10 min. • Cook: 7 min.

1 (18¹/₂-ounce) package hoagie
   rolls, split
3 tablespoons extra-virgin olive oil
1 (4¹/₂-ounce) can chopped ripe
   olives, drained
6 plum tomatoes, thinly sliced
6 ounces Gruyère cheese, sliced
1/3 cup coarsely chopped fresh basil

1. Lightly brush cut sides of rolls with oil; sprinkle evenly with olives. Top with tomato slices, cheese, and basil.
2. Grill rolls, cut sides up, over *Direct Medium* heat until cheese melts, about 5 to 7 minutes. Yield: 6 servings.

Light-as-a-Cloud Biscuits

Prep: 15 min. • Cook: 14 min.

1/3 cup unsalted butter
2 cups self-rising soft wheat flour
³/₄ cup buttermilk
Unsalted butter, melted

1. Cut 1/3 cup butter into flour with a pastry blender until crumbly. Add buttermilk, stirring until dry ingredients are moistened.
2. Turn dough out onto a lightly floured surface; knead 3 or 4 times.
3. Roll dough to ³/₄-inch thickness; cut with a 2½-inch round cutter, and place on a baking sheet.
4. Bake biscuits at 425°F for 12 to 14 minutes. Brush with melted butter. Yield: 8 biscuits.

Sour Cream Crescent Rolls

Prep: 31 min. • Cook: 10 min. • Other: 8¹/₂ hrs.

1/2 cup unsalted butter
1 (8-ounce) container sour cream
1/2 cup sugar
2 (¹/₄-ounce) envelopes active
   dry yeast
1/2 cup warm water (100°F to 110°F)
2 large eggs, beaten
4 cups all-purpose flour
1 teaspoon salt
Unsalted butter, melted

1. Melt ½ cup butter in a saucepan over medium heat; stir in sour cream and sugar, and heat to 100°F to 110°F.
2. Combine yeast and warm water in a 1-cup liquid measuring cup; let stand 5 minutes.
3. Combine yeast mixture, sour cream mixture, and eggs in a large bowl. Combine flour and salt; gradually add to yeast mixture, stirring well. Cover and store in refrigerator at least 8 hours or up to 24 hours.
4. Punch dough down; divide into 4 equal portions. Roll each portion into a 10-inch circle on a floured surface; brush with melted butter. Cut each circle into 12 wedges; roll up each wedge, beginning at wide end. Place on greased baking sheets, point side down.
5. Cover and let rise in a warm place (85°F), free from drafts, 30 minutes or until doubled in bulk. Bake at 375°F for 10 minutes or until golden. Yield: 4 dozen.

Spicy Breadsticks

Spicy Breadsticks

Prep: 15 min. • Cook: 12 min.

These crisp breadsticks are perfect for pairing with simple grilled meats. If you can't find seasoned pepper blend, combine equal portions of cracked black pepper, red bell pepper flakes, and salt. Store in an airtight container.

1 (11-ounce) can refrigerated soft breadsticks
1 large egg, lightly beaten
2 tablespoons paprika
2 tablespoons seasoned pepper blend

1. Separate breadsticks; working with 2 at a time, roll each breadstick into a 12-inch rope. Brush ropes with egg. Twist ropes together, pinching ends to seal. Repeat with the remaining breadsticks.
2. Combine paprika and pepper blend; spread mixture on a paper plate. Roll breadsticks in pepper mixture, pressing gently to coat. (Wash hands between rolling each breadstick, if necessary.)
3. Place breadsticks on a lightly greased baking sheet. Bake at 375°F for 10 to 12 minutes. Yield: 4 servings.

best bread tips

It happens sometimes. You can't use your bread fast enough, and it goes stale. Try this: Sprinkle stale bread with water, wrap it in foil, and bake at 350°F until warm and soft. Or, place individual slices on a splatter screen and hold them over a pan of simmering water for a minute or two.

perfect summer sweets

Take your pick from five desserts from the grill and crowd-pleasing desserts you can make ahead indoors.

Grilled Banana-Walnut Quesadillas

DIRECT • MEDIUM
Prep: 10 min. • Cook: 1 min.

2 tablespoons granulated sugar
1/2 teaspoon ground cinnamon
1/8 teaspoon ground nutmeg
4 (8-inch) flour tortillas
Extra-virgin olive oil
2 cups coarsely chopped banana
2 teaspoons lemon juice
1/4 cup chopped walnuts, toasted
1 cup frozen vanilla yogurt
1/4 cup caramel topping
Garnish: fresh thyme blossom
    (optional)

1. Combine first 3 ingredients in a small bowl; set aside.
2. Lightly brush or spray 1 side of each tortilla with oil; sprinkle oiled sides evenly with 1 tablespoon sugar mixture.
3. Combine banana, lemon juice, and remaining sugar mixture; toss gently. Spoon banana mixture evenly over half of each plain side of tortillas. Sprinkle walnuts over the banana mixture.
4. Grill the tortillas, oiled sides down, over *Direct Medium* heat until bottoms of tortillas are golden, about 30 seconds. Fold each tortilla in half; grill until thoroughly heated, about 30 seconds more.
5. Remove quesadillas from grill. Spoon 1/4 cup frozen yogurt onto each quesadilla; drizzle caramel topping evenly over top. Garnish, if desired. Yield: 4 servings.

Grilled Pound Cake with Peach Sauce

DIRECT • MEDIUM
Prep: 5 min. • Cook: 2 min.

1 (16-ounce) package frozen
    peaches, thawed, or 3 cups
    sliced fresh peaches
1/4 cup honey
1/2 teaspoon almond extract
1 (16-ounce) loaf pound cake
Extra-virgin olive oil
1 cup frozen whipped topping,
    thawed

1. Combine first 3 ingredients; set aside.
2. Cut cake into 8 slices. Lightly brush or spray slices with oil. Grill slices over *Direct Medium* heat until toasted, 1 to 2 minutes, turning once.
3. Place 1 cake slice on each of 8 individual serving plates. Top cake slices evenly with peach mixture and whipped topping. Yield: 8 servings.

---

dessert by the pound

The dessert above is made extra-easy by using a store-bought pound cake. However, for the absolute best flavor, try making your own pound cake to slice and grill. Let the cake cool completely before cutting into slices approximately 1/2- to 1-inch thick. Then follow the recipe as directed.

S'mores

DIRECT • HIGH
Prep: 5 min. • Cook: 2 min.

No need to hold out for a camping trip to enjoy these marshmallow treats. After grilling dinner, turn the heat to High and gather 'round to roast the marshmallows.

8 graham crackers, halved
4 (1 1/2-ounce) chocolate candy
    bars, halved
Long sticks or skewers
16 large marshmallows

1. Top half of graham crackers with a chocolate bar half.
2. Insert sticks through marshmallows; hold marshmallows over *Direct High* heat (but not touching the grate) until browned, about 2 minutes, turning occasionally. Place 2 roasted marshmallows on each chocolate bar half; top with remaining graham crackers. Yield: 8 servings.

Peanut Butter S'mores:

1. Spread 1 tablespoon peanut butter each on half of graham crackers. Top with chocolate bar halves; proceed as directed.

Toffee Bits S'mores:

1. Sprinkle 1 teaspoon toffee bits over each chocolate-topped graham cracker, and proceed as directed.

Grilled Banana-Walnut
Quesadillas

Ginger Grilled Pineapple with Ice Cream

Ginger Grilled Pineapple with Ice Cream

DIRECT • MEDIUM

Prep: 12 min. • Cook: 12 min.

Save time and buy pineapple already peeled and cored from your supermarket's produce section.

1 pineapple, peeled
3 tablespoons light brown sugar
$^1/_2$ teaspoon ground cinnamon
1 tablespoon grated fresh ginger
Extra-virgin olive oil
Vanilla ice cream
Ground cinnamon

1. Cut pineapple in half lengthwise; remove and discard core. Combine brown sugar, cinnamon, and ginger; rub all over the pineapple.
2. Lightly brush or spray pineapple with oil. Grill the pineapple over *Direct Medium* heat until lightly browned, 10 to 12 minutes, turning once. Remove pineapple from grill; cut into $^1/_4$-inch slices. Serve with ice cream; sprinkle lightly with cinnamon. Yield: 6 servings.

Grilled Pear Fantasia

DIRECT • MEDIUM

Prep: 6 min. • Cook: 10 min.

3 firm, ripe, unpeeled pears
3 tablespoons honey
2 tablespoons fresh orange juice
$^3/_4$ cup seedless raspberry jam, melted
$1^1/_2$ cups frozen vanilla yogurt

1. Cut each pear in half lengthwise; remove and discard core. Combine honey and orange juice; brush some of the honey mixture over cut surfaces of pear halves, reserving remaining honey mixture.
2. Grill the pears over *Direct Medium* heat until tender, 8 to 10 minutes, turning occasionally and basting with remaining honey mixture. While pears grill, spoon raspberry jam into a small saucepan; cook over low heat, stirring constantly, until melted.
3. Place hot or room temperature pear halves onto 6 individual plates. Top each with 2 tablespoons melted raspberry jam and $^1/_4$ cup frozen yogurt. Yield: 6 servings.

Butter-Mint Shortbread

Prep: 10 min. • Cook: 20 min. • Other: 10 min.

These cookies are like a dessert and after-dinner mint in one.

1 cup unsalted butter, softened
$^3/_4$ cup powdered sugar
$^1/_2$ teaspoon mint extract
$^1/_2$ teaspoon vanilla extract
2 cups all-purpose flour
Powdered sugar

1. Beat the butter and $^3/_4$ cup powdered sugar at medium speed with an electric mixer until light and fluffy. Add the extracts, beating until blended. Gradually add the flour, beating at low speed until blended after each addition. Pat the dough into a 15- x 10-inch rectangle on a large baking sheet lined with parchment paper.

2. Bake at 325°F for 18 to 20 minutes or until lightly browned. Cool in pan on a wire rack 10 minutes. Cut into squares; sprinkle with powdered sugar. Remove from pan; cool on wire rack. Yield: 3 dozen.

Double-Frosted Bourbon Brownies

Prep: 12 min. • Cook: 35 min.

³/₄ cup all-purpose flour
¹/₄ teaspoon baking soda
¹/₄ teaspoon salt
¹/₂ cup sugar
¹/₃ cup shortening
2 tablespoons water
1 cup (6 ounces) semisweet
   chocolate morsels
1 teaspoon vanilla extract
2 large eggs
1¹/₂ cups chopped walnuts
¹/₄ cup bourbon
White Frosting
Chocolate Glaze

1. Combine first 3 ingredients in a medium bowl; stir well. Set flour mixture aside.
2. Combine sugar and shortening in a medium saucepan. Cook over low heat, stirring constantly until shortening melts and mixture is blended; remove from heat. Add water, chocolate morsels, and vanilla, stirring until smooth. Add

eggs, 1 at a time, stirring after each addition. Add dry ingredients and walnuts; stir well. Spoon into a greased 9-inch square pan. Bake at 325°F for 30 minutes or until a wooden pick inserted in center comes out clean.

3. Sprinkle bourbon evenly over warm brownies. Cool completely in pan on a wire rack. Spread White Frosting on brownies. Pour warm Chocolate Glaze over frosting. Let stand until set. Cut into squares. Yield: 16 large brownies or 2¹/₂ dozen small brownies.

White Frosting

Prep: 5 min.

¹/₂ cup unsalted butter, softened
1 teaspoon vanilla extract
2 cups sifted powdered sugar

1. Combine butter and vanilla in a large mixing bowl; beat at medium speed with an electric mixer until creamy. Gradually add powdered sugar, beating until smooth. Yield: 1¹/₄ cups.

Chocolate Glaze

Prep: 5 min. • Cook: 10 min.

1 cup (6 ounces) semisweet
   chocolate morsels
1 tablespoon shortening

1. Combine chocolate morsels and shortening in a small heavy saucepan. Cook over low heat until chocolate morsels melt, stirring occasionally. Yield: ¹/₂ cup.

Best-Ever Lemon Bars

Best-Ever Lemon Bars

Prep: 15 min. • Cook: 50 min.

These shortbread-based bars contain just the right amount of tangy lemon filling. Try cutting them with a heart-shaped cookie cutter instead of into bars for a special touch.

2¹/₄ cups all-purpose flour, divided
¹/₂ cup sifted powdered sugar
1 cup unsalted butter
¹/₂ teaspoon baking powder
4 large eggs, lightly beaten
2 cups granulated sugar
¹/₃ cup lemon juice
Sifted powdered sugar

1. Combine 2 cups flour and ¹/₂ cup powdered sugar; cut in butter with a pastry blender until mixture is crumbly. Firmly press mixture into a greased 13- x 9-inch pan. Bake at 350°F for 20 to 25 minutes or until lightly browned.
2. Combine remaining ¹/₄ cup flour and baking powder in a small bowl; stir well. Combine eggs, 2 cups granulated sugar, and lemon juice in a large bowl; stir in flour mixture. Pour over prepared crust. Bake at 350°F for 25 minutes or until set and lightly browned. Cool completely in pan on a wire rack. Sprinkle with additional powdered sugar; cut into bars. Yield: 2¹/₂ dozen.

Double-Frosted Bourbon Brownies

Fresh-Fruit Pizza with Lemon Sauce

Prep: 23 min. • Cook: 13 min.

1 (18-ounce) package refrigerated
   sugar cookie dough
2 tablespoons seedless raspberry
   jam, melted
$^2/_3$ cup Lemon Sauce
2 cups fresh raspberries
2 cups fresh blackberries
2 cup sliced fresh strawberries

1. Press cookie dough into a 12-inch pizza pan coated with cooking spray. Bake at 350°F for 13 minutes or until golden brown. Cool completely on a wire rack.
2. Spread jam over crust. Spread Lemon Sauce over jam; arrange raspberries, blackberries, and strawberry slices on top. Serve immediately. Yield: 12 servings.

Lemon Sauce

Prep: 6 min. • Cook: 7 min. • Other: 1 hr.

$^3/_4$ cup sugar
1 tablespoon grated lemon zest
2 large eggs
$^2/_3$ cup fresh lemon juice (about
   3 large lemons)
3 tablespoons unsalted butter

1. Combine first 3 ingredients in a saucepan over medium heat, stirring with a wire whisk. Cook until sugar dissolves and mixture is light in color (about 3 minutes).
2. Stir in lemon juice and butter; cook 4 minutes or until mixture thinly coats back of a spoon, stirring constantly with whisk. Cool. Cover and chill (mixture will thicken as it cools). Yield: 1⅓ cups.

Note: Lemon Sauce can be stored in the refrigerator up to 1 week. You can easily double the recipe and freeze half of it. Thaw in the refrigerator; use within 1 week.

Apple Shortbread Crisp

Prep: 7 min. • Cook: 36 min.

The buttery, crispy shortbread cookie topping on this dessert will leave you wanting more.

2 (12-ounce) packages frozen
   apple chunks (we used
   Stouffer's® Harvest Apples)
6 tablespoons unsalted butter
20 shortbread cookies, crushed
   (we used Keebler® Sandies
   Simply Shortbread)
$^1/_2$ cup chopped walnuts
$^1/_4$ cup firmly packed light brown
   sugar
1 teaspoon ground cinnamon,
   divided
$^1/_4$ teaspoon ground nutmeg
2 tablespoons light brown sugar
Vanilla ice cream

1. Prick plastic wrap covering apple chunks several times with a fork; microwave at MEDIUM (50% power) 7 minutes or until apple is thawed. Let stand 2 minutes.

2. Meanwhile, melt butter in a large skillet over medium heat; add cookie crumbs and walnuts. Cook, stirring constantly, 2 minutes. Remove from heat, and stir in ¼ cup brown sugar, ½ teaspoon cinnamon, and nutmeg.

3. Combine 2 tablespoons brown sugar and remaining ½ teaspoon cinnamon; sprinkle in a lightly greased 1-quart baking dish. Sprinkle half of apple over brown sugar mixture; top with half of cookie crumb mixture. Repeat layers with remaining apple and crumb mixture.

4. Bake at 375°F for 25 minutes or until golden. Serve warm with vanilla ice cream. Yield: 6 servings.

Colossal Chocolate Chip Cookies

(pictured on page 111)

Prep: 20 min. • Cook: 10 min.

If you don't have a heavy-duty stand mixer to handle this amount of dough, cut the recipe in half.

2 cups unsalted butter, softened
2 cups granulated sugar
2 cups firmly packed brown sugar
4 large eggs
2 teaspoons vanilla extract
4 cups all-purpose flour
2 teaspoons baking powder
2 teaspoons baking soda
1 teaspoon salt
5 cups regular oats,
    uncooked
3 cups (18 ounces) semisweet
    chocolate morsels
1 (7-ounce) milk chocolate candy
    bar, coarsely chopped
2 cups chopped walnuts

1. Beat butter at medium speed with a heavy-duty electric mixer until creamy; gradually add sugars, beating well. Add eggs and vanilla; beat well.

2. Combine flour and next 3 ingredients; gradually add to butter mixture, beating well.

3. Process oats in a food processor until finely ground. Gradually add to butter mixture, beating

well. Stir in chocolate morsels, chopped chocolate, and walnuts.

4. Shape cookie dough into 2-inch balls. Place 3 inches apart on ungreased baking sheets. Flatten each ball into a 2½-inch circle. Bake at 375°F for 8 to 10 minutes or until lightly browned. Cool slightly on baking sheets; remove to wire racks to cool completely. Yield: 4 dozen.

Lemon Buttermilk Cake with Lemon Butter Sauce

Prep: 25 min. • Cook: 1 hr. • Other: 10 min.

Attention, lemon lovers: This is your dream dessert.

1 cup butter, softened
2¹⁄₃ cups granulated sugar,
    divided
3 large eggs
3 cups all-purpose flour
¹⁄₂ teaspoon baking soda
¹⁄₂ teaspoon salt
1 cup buttermilk
1¹⁄₂ tablespoons grated lemon
    zest
¹⁄₂ cup plus 3 tablespoons fresh
    lemon juice, divided
3 tablespoons fine, dry
    breadcrumbs
Powdered sugar (optional)
Lemon Butter Sauce

1. Beat butter at medium speed with an electric mixer until creamy; gradually add 2 cups granulated sugar, beating well. Add eggs, 1 at a time, beating after each addition.

2. Combine flour, baking soda, and salt; add to butter mixture alternately with buttermilk, beginning and ending with flour mixture. Mix at low speed after each addition until blended. Stir in zest and 3 tablespoons juice. Pour into a buttered 12-cup Bundt pan coated with breadcrumbs. Bake at 350°F for 55 minutes or until a wooden pick inserted in center comes out clean. Cool in pan on a wire rack 10 minutes; remove from pan, and place on a wire rack.

3. Combine remaining ¹⁄₃ cup granulated sugar and ½ cup lemon juice in a saucepan; cook over medium-low heat until sugar dissolves, stirring often. Prick cake at 1-inch intervals with a long wooden skewer or cake tester. Spoon juice mixture over warm cake; cool completely on wire rack. Dust with powdered sugar, if desired. Serve with Lemon Butter Sauce. Yield: one 10-inch cake.

Lemon Butter Sauce

Prep: 8 min. • Cook: 10 min.

2 cups sugar
6 large eggs, lightly beaten
¹⁄₄ cup grated lemon zest
³⁄₄ cup fresh lemon juice
³⁄₄ cup butter, softened

1. Combine first 4 ingredients in top of a double boiler; bring water to a boil. Reduce heat to medium; cook, stirring constantly, until mixture coats a spoon. Cool slightly. Add butter, 1 tablespoon at a time, whisking until blended. Serve immediately, or cover and refrigerate until ready to serve. Yield: 4 cups.

saucy tips

The Lemon Butter Sauce above is a great secret to have in your fridge. Not only is it delicious with slices of Lemon Buttermilk Cake, you can drizzle it over a grocery store cake as well. Keep a small loaf of pound cake in the freezer and you'll be ready for any drop-in guests. Or, for even less fuss, serve this sauce over scoops of vanilla ice cream.

Berry-Amaretto Summer
Trifle Parfaits

Berry-Amaretto Summer Trifle Parfaits

Prep: 15 min. • Other: 2 hrs., 10 min.

Any combination of berries will work in this stunning trifle. Use what's freshest in your area.

1 1/2 cups sliced strawberries
3/4 cup blueberries
2 tablespoons almond liqueur
1 cup frozen whipped topping, thawed
1 1/2 cups (1-inch) cubed angel food cake
2 tablespoons frozen whipped topping, thawed

1. Combine first 3 ingredients in a medium bowl; stir gently. Let stand 10 minutes.
2. Spoon 1/3 cup berry mixture into each of 2 (12-ounce) parfait glasses, and top each with 1/4 cup whipped topping and about 1/3 cup cake cubes. Repeat layers with remaining ingredients, ending with berry mixture. Cover and chill 2 hours. Top each parfait with 1 tablespoon whipped topping before serving. Yield: 2 servings.

Italian Cream Cheese Cake

Prep: 20 min. • Cook: 35 min. • Other: 10 min.

This lofty layer cake is sure to appeal to anyone who dreams of coconut, cream cheese, and pecans.

1 cup unsalted butter, softened
2 cups sugar
5 large eggs, separated
2 cups all-purpose flour
1 teaspoon baking soda
1/4 teaspoon salt
1 cup buttermilk
1 teaspoon vanilla extract
1 cup chopped pecans
1 cup flaked coconut
Cream Cheese Frosting

1. Beat butter at medium speed with an electric mixer until creamy; gradually add sugar, beating well. Add egg yolks, 1 at a time, beating after each addition.
2. Combine flour, baking soda, and salt; add to butter mixture alternately with buttermilk, beginning and ending with flour mixture. Mix at low speed after each addition until blended. Stir in vanilla. Add pecans and coconut; stir well.
3. Beat egg whites at high speed until stiff peaks form. Gently fold into batter. Spoon batter into 2 greased and floured 9-inch round cakepans. Bake at 350°F for 30 to 35 minutes or until a wooden pick inserted in center comes out clean. Cool in pans on wire racks 10 minutes; remove from pans, and cool completely on wire racks.
4. Spread Cream Cheese Frosting between layers and on top and sides of cake. Cover and store in refrigerator. Yield: one 2-layer cake.

Cream Cheese Frosting

Prep: 5 min.

1 (8-ounce) package cream cheese, softened
1/2 cup unsalted butter, softened
1 (16-ounce) package powdered sugar
1 cup chopped pecans, toasted
1 teaspoon vanilla extract

1. Beat cream cheese and butter at medium speed with an electric mixer until creamy; gradually add sugar, beating until smooth. Stir in pecans and vanilla. Yield: 3 1/2 cups.

Frozen Chocolate-Macadamia Nut Pie

Prep: 25 min. • Cook: 2 min.

Other: 4 hrs., 10 min.

1 cup (6 ounces) semisweet chocolate morsels
1 2/3 cups crushed chocolate wafers (6 ounces)
1/4 cup unsalted butter, melted
1/2 (8-ounce) package cream cheese, softened
3/4 cup sugar
1 1/2 teaspoons vanilla extract
1 (3 1/2-ounce) jar macadamia nuts, coarsely chopped
2 cups whipping cream

1. Place chocolate morsels in a heavy saucepan over low heat until chocolate melts, stirring often. Remove from heat, and set aside.
2. Combine crushed wafers and butter. Firmly press mixture into bottom of a lightly buttered 9-inch springform pan.
3. Combine melted chocolate, cream cheese, sugar, and vanilla in a mixing bowl; beat at medium speed with an electric mixer until smooth. Fold in macadamia nuts.
4. Beat 2 cups whipping cream at high speed with an electric mixer until soft peaks form. Add about one-fourth of whipped cream to chocolate mixture, and beat until blended. Fold remaining whipped cream into chocolate mixture. Pour into crust. Cover and freeze 4 hours or until firm.
5. To serve, carefully remove sides of pan; let pie stand 10 minutes before serving. Yield: one 9-inch pie.

Butter Pecan Ice Cream

Prep: 15 min. • Cook: 12 min. • Other: 1 hr.

3/4 cup firmly packed brown sugar
1/2 cup water
1/8 teaspoon salt
2 large eggs, lightly beaten
2 tablespoons butter
1 cup milk
1 teaspoon vanilla extract
1 cup whipping cream
1/2 cup finely chopped pecans, toasted

1. Combine first 3 ingredients in top of a double boiler; bring water to a boil. Reduce heat to low; cook, stirring constantly, 3 to 4 minutes or until sugar dissolves. Gradually stir a small amount of hot mixture into eggs; add to remaining hot mixture, stirring constantly. Cook over medium heat, stirring constantly, until thermometer registers 160°F and mixture thickens (about 4 to 5 minutes). Remove from heat; stir in butter, and let cool. Stir in milk and remaining ingredients.
2. Pour mixture into freezer container of a 2-quart hand-turned or electric freezer. Freeze according to manufacturer's instructions.
3. Pack freezer with additional ice and rock salt, and let stand 1 hour before serving. Yield: 1 quart.

Pecan Pie Bars

Prep: 15 min. • Cook: 55 min.

2 cups all-purpose flour
1/2 cup granulated sugar
1/8 teaspoon salt
3/4 cup unsalted butter, cut up
1 cup firmly packed light brown sugar
1 cup light corn syrup
1/2 cup unsalted butter
4 large eggs, lightly beaten
2 1/2 cups finely chopped pecans
1 teaspoon vanilla extract

1. Combine flour, granulated sugar, and salt in a large bowl; cut in 3/4 cup butter thoroughly with a pastry blender until mixture resembles very fine crumbs.
2. Press mixture evenly into a greased 13- x 9-inch pan, using a piece of plastic wrap to press crumb mixture firmly in pan. Bake at 350°F for 17 to 20 minutes or until lightly browned.
3. Combine brown sugar, corn syrup, and 1/2 cup butter in a saucepan; bring to a boil over medium heat, stirring gently. Remove from heat.
4. Stir one-fourth of hot mixture into beaten eggs; add to remaining hot mixture. Stir in pecans and vanilla. Pour filling over crust.
5. Bake at 350°F for 34 to 35 minutes or until set. Cool completely in pan on a wire rack. Cut into bars. Yield: 16 large bars.

Warm Fudge-Filled Cheesecake

Prep: 20 min. • Cook: 1 1/4 hrs. • Other: 1 hr.

Plan for this cheesecake to come hot from the oven about the time you sit down to dinner, and it will cool down to a nice warm, fudgy consistency when you're ready to enjoy it.

1/2 cup unsalted butter, softened
1/3 cup sugar
1 cup all-purpose flour
1 tablespoon vanilla extract, divided
2/3 cup chopped pistachios
4 (8-ounce) packages cream cheese, softened
1 1/2 cups sugar
4 large eggs
2 cups (12 ounces) semisweet chocolate mini-morsels
Sweetened whipped cream

1. Beat butter at medium speed with an electric mixer until creamy; add 1/3 cup sugar, beating well. Gradually add flour, and beat at low speed until blended. Stir in 1 teaspoon vanilla and pistachios. Press into bottom and 1 1/2 inches up sides of a 9-inch springform pan.
2. Bake at 350°F for 12 to 15 minutes or until golden. Cool on a wire rack.
3. Beat cream cheese at medium speed with an electric mixer until light and fluffy; gradually add 1 1/2 cups sugar, beating well. Add eggs, 1 at a time, beating just until yellow disappears. Stir in remaining 2 teaspoons vanilla (do not overmix).
4. Pour half of batter into crust; sprinkle with chocolate morsels to within 3/4 inch of edge. Pour in remaining batter, starting at outer edge and working toward center. Place cheesecake on a baking sheet.
5. Bake at 350°F for 1 hour or until set. Cool on a wire rack 1 hour. Serve slightly warm with sweetened whipped cream. Yield: 12 servings.

Recipe Index